COLORS OF THE WORLD

THE GEOGRAPHY OF COLOR

JEAN-PHILIPPE LENCLOS

DOMINIQUE LENCLOS

COLORS OF THE WORLD

THE GEOGRAPHY OF COLOR

PREFACE BY FRANÇOIS BARRÉ

TRANSLATED BY GREGORY P. BRUHN

W. W. NORTON & COMPANY

NEW YORK · LONDON

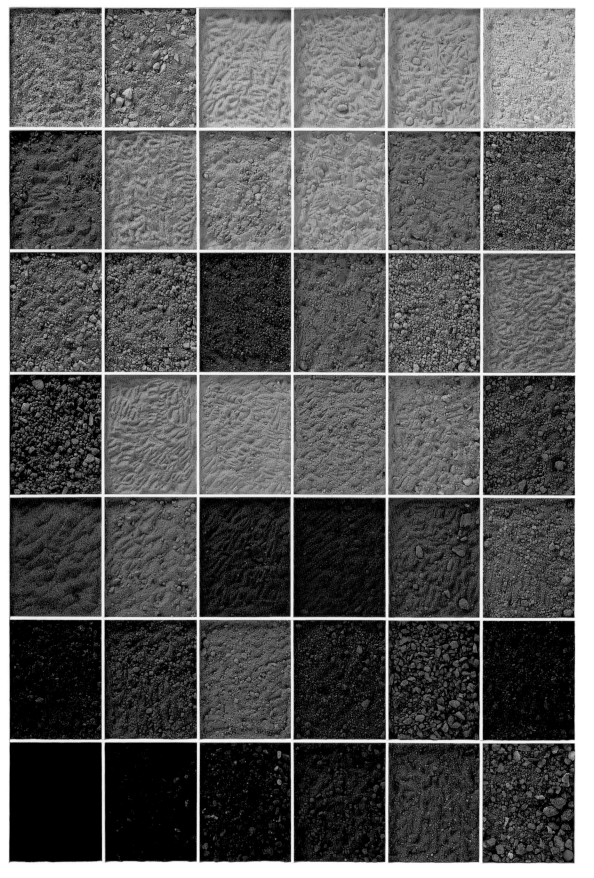

These forty-two soil samples, collected from the four corners of the globe, express a whole variety of natural soil colors dominated by yellowish and reddish ochre, a coloration caused by the presence of iron oxides. The various site analyses presented in this text focus on the fundamental importance of soil matter throughout Africa, Asia, the Middle East, and Latin America.

Copyright © 1999 by Groupe Moniteur (Editions le Moniteur), Paris
English translation copyright © 2004 by W. W. Norton & Company, Inc.

Originally published in French as COULEURS DU MONDE: Géographie de la Couleur

All rights reserved
Printed in Italy

For information about permission to reproduce selections from this book, write to Permissions, W. W. Norton & Company, Inc., 500 Fifth Avenue, New York, NY 10110

Manufacturing by Rotolito Lombarda
Book design by Peter Keller
Composition by Ken Gross

Library of Congress Cataloging-in-Publication Data

Lenclos, Jean-Philippe
   [Couleurs du monde. English] Colors of the world : the geography of color / Jean-Philippe Lenclos, Dominique Lenclos; preface by François Barré; translated by Gregory P. Bruhn.
              p.   cm.
       Includes bibliographical references.
       ISBN 0-393-73147-2
1. Color in architecture. 2. Vernacular architecture. 3. Dwellings. I. Lenclos, Dominique. II. Title.

NA2795.L42513	2004
729'.4—dc22	2003059354

W. W. Norton & Company, Inc.,
500 Fifth Avenue, New York, N.Y. 10110

www.wwnorton.com

W. W. Norton & Company Ltd.,
Castle House, 75/76 Wells St., London W1T 3QT

0 9 8 7 6 5 4 3 2

FOREWORD

DOMINIQUE LENCLOS

Colors of the World is a new work devoted to the colors of popular habitats. It presents a dozen site studies completed in the four corners of the world, and gives an idea of the diversity with which a chromatic physiognomy is presented in city, town, and country homes in a given region of the Maghreb (Morocco, Algeria, and Tunisia), Latin America, or South America.

Every habitat is colored, whether earthen, like the skyscrapers in the city of Shibam in Yemen, or whitewashed, like the houses of the *pueblos blancos* in Andalusia. You may wonder why we are interested in one site over another. Certain subjects are compelling on their own, since they seem to correspond to our objectives: geographical situation, homogeneity of architectural character, and specific chromatic expression of a given region or country. It is often chance that guides us: One day, looking through a publication, we found an article on the traditional costumes of the inhabitants of Karpathos; but, in terms of background décor, the houses were polychromatic—it was this photo that convinced us to travel to the Greek island, an analysis of which is included in *Colors of Europe.* During our on-site examinations, we also occasionally come upon an unexpected subject of study: While working on the Ndebele paintings of South Africa, we discovered the Sotho décors, which demonstrate an admirable diversity and creativity, though they are not widely known.

It is important to observe that it is rarely the inhabitants of a country who allow us to make these discoveries. In fact, most of the time, they do not perceive the chromatic specificity of their daily environment, whose palette is the fruit of old customs and spontaneous creation; they have a hard time conceiving why foreigners are interested in a habitat that they judge to be modest and that they dream of replacing with a modern house. In the course of our investigations, when we stop in front of an ensemble that seems particularly interesting, we are sometimes perceived as imaginative or enlightened. Moreover, in France, we have been questioned many times by the police, alerted by villagers who found it suspicious that we were collecting detailed samples of their homes.

Our works, for those who read them, and our methods for the studied sites, for those who live there, will perhaps help either group to become conscious of the fact that the color of a habitat is a wealth that they possess and for which they are responsible, and that they can contribute to the quality of the environment.

Certain site analyses presented in this book were conducted under difficult conditions—in 1984, when we went to Guatemala, the country was torn apart by guerillas, for example. Other countries are currently no longer accessible; still others have turned a page in their history.

These studies, each one dated, are objective assessments of the chromatic state of a site at a given time. For those who consider color to be an inseparable element of architectural and cultural heritage, they offer cultural and historical insight and can serve as the foundation for future research on the evolution of taste and usage in the field of color.

We have noted that, in numerous countries, public authorities have become aware of the fact that the color of a locale plays an important role in the landscape and that, similar to monuments and art, it belongs to the cultural heritage of a city or region. This awareness has often resulted in the establishment of local regulations aimed at promoting the quality of architecture and at defining the color palettes designed for new construction and for the rehabilitation of older habitats. In France, these regulations date back to the 1970s; they are older in England for protected sites such as Cambridge or Oxford, and even older in Italy, where, in 1808, Napoleon I imposed the creation of a guiding outline for the application of color in the city of Turin!

In the course of our travels, we often have the chance to take note of how much the renovation of an old neighborhood and its revaluation through color restore life to places that have become pitiful, always on condition that the color palette chosen is neither too artificial nor too reductive. We observe with great interest, and often surprise, as was the case in Pernambuco, the impact that an urban coloration outline can have, in the most natural and spontaneous manner, on surrounding villages and even on particular habitations. The palette defined by the colorist or architect is assimilated, interpreted by the inhabitant who then uniquely transforms and recreates it, according to fancy, originality, a momentary mood, and personal taste.

Faced with the danger of a universal and uniform culture, this tour along the horizon of colors in the popular habitat, as partial and insufficient as it may be, seeks to shed light, appropriately, on the role of color in the specific cultural identity of every country and people the world over.

Dominique Lenclos

ACKNOWLEDGMENTS

Thank you to everyone who has helped us to bring
this long research to term.

First, and very warmly, Christian des Garets and
Michel Sarmont who, through their enlightened
advice and faithful friendship, have always
encouraged and helped us in our undertaking.

We also wish to express our deep gratitude to our
friend, professor, and researcher Song Jian Ming
who, through his numerous publications on color,
has made our work and research widely known in
China.

Thank you particularly to Peter Keller. Through his
creative talent and admirable attention to detail, he
has once again ensured the selection of documents,
the makeup and the typography of this text, the
third step of our "pilgrimage" into the countryside
of color.

Thank you also to Fabrice Moireau who, through
his consummate art as a watercolorist, illustrated
each of the sites studied.

Thanks also to Rudi Meyer who added his expert
opinion in the conception of the cartographic
illustrations of countries, as well as to René Robert
who always knew how to assume the delicate task
of sample reproduction and synthesis work with
remarkable precision.

We would like to warmly and specially thank
Professor Andreï Efimov, Professor Mohammad
Hossein Halimi, as well as Eiji Ogawa, the president
of the Color Planning Center in Tokyo, and
Professor Shingo Yoshida who, through his valued
assistance and deep knowledge of places and
cultures, helped us discover the cities of Suzdal,
Yazd, and Murotsu.

A big thank you as well to all of the members of
Atelier 3D Couleur and friends who actively
participated in this work: Marie Fournier, Philippe
Roaldès, Marie Lenclos, Agnès Decourchelle,
Béatrice Kluge, Christophe Roger, Michiyo Mori,
Thomas Klug, Tom Porter, François Dejean,
Isabelle Jacquard, Jean Bersoux, Mariù Gondim,
Patricia Vasconcellos, Anne Laurence, Brahim
Madaci, as well as the painter Ryoichi Shigeta. We
equally express all of our gratitude to Fabienne
Gindre for her constant assistance, her devotion,
and her tireless patience.

Finally, thank you to all of the known and
unknown inhabitants, architects, and artisans
whom the beauty of the habitat and landscape
colors recalls; as such, they participate in a
continued and lively manner in the history and
geography of color.

For Lucie Long

TABLE OF CONTENTS

PREFACE

FRANÇOIS BARRÉ

National Director of Architecture
Department of French Cultural Ministry, 1999

Colors of the World, Colors of Time

I discovered Jean-Philippe Lenclos' work in 1967 at the Salon des Artistes Décorateurs, where, under the aegis of Domus, he was presenting an auditorium for a cultural center or university which seemed to me a new approach in color, at once sensible and spectacular (during this period, "supergraphism" was being invented). Since then, I have not stopped following the extraordinary journey he has undertaken with Dominique, his wife, which has led them around the world. Having left the light of the North and its wild harmonies, Jean-Philippe discovered in Japan, at the age of twenty-two, the subtle combinations of color and their relationships to culture, identity, and history. In the shadow of Tanizaki and before Balthus confirmed a few years later, at the Villa Medici, that "In painting, everything is a play between hot and cold," he began to forge a new idea in color and to put it to work at the heart of his agency, Atelier 3D Couleur. The spectrum he has traversed is extremely broad since, with the passing of time, Lenclos has taken on the automobile, the cycle, architecture, planes, pens, textiles, and a firm's painting strategy (Gauthier)—thus remaining interested in everything that derives from the conception and application of color in environment, architecture, and industrial products. Only fashion, with its artifice and programmed moves, was kept at a distance from his endless curiosity, for it was a question of being essential.

The geography of color expresses the consciousness of an ancient and memorable tale that research— this workshop of lengthy patience, approximating Le Corbusier—literally allows to be revealed. The vocabulary of color is so anchored in the memory of soils, in the proximity and use of materials, in beliefs and symbols, in relations to the sky, to light, to the climate, to passing time—like passing colors—that often we no longer know how to see or explain what is before our eyes. For thirty years, the Lenclos have consequently been inventing a previously unknown discipline.

This book is neither a travel diary nor passionate love chronicle, nor is it a surveyor's notebook or even an infinite display of a zealous scrutinizer. It's all of these at once, interweaving pleasure and method. After *Colors of France* and *Colors of Europe*, here, then, are the *Colors of the World*. It is no coincidence that this work is being done today, that these books are being published in France, in Japan, in Korea, etc. and that similar works are underway in numerous countries—China, Japan, Portugal, Norway, Finland (where Lenclos participated in the first post-secondary-level instruction on color).

It is in fact important to defend our colors, so to speak, in a peaceful manner. At the dawn of globalization, everyone must know what he or she is in order to better participate in the general conference. This "conference" will only be of interest if we can maintain within it our singularities, our tastes, our knowledge, and our culture, without refusing to profit from a potentially beautiful exposure to the world. Only knowledge can expose us to exchange without forcing us into nostalgic positions or hurling us into an oblivion of what has made us. The disciplinary support that comes from the geography of color is that much more indispensable when color's status remains ambiguous: at once a changing and reversible value that we can easily recover in order to play with various identities and facile seductions, yet also a slow and profound stratification of time and space.

The Lenclos allow us to follow an outlined path without being traditionalists, and to imagine the future without being forgetful. They understand the frailty of everything they have seen and how many threats exist which, more than sunlight or sea spray, risk reducing color to a final cosmetic recourse in city landscapes. It is in this way that they have been able to take note of contradictory influences that seem nevertheless to suggest a singular will of distinction. Often, popular tradition vanishes in a sort of generalized white-washing. Within a couple of years, the Greek village of Menetes has lost its blues and turquoises in favor of whites and light ochres. Conversely the elected officials are fond of bright colors and ascribe imaginary qualities of image and immediate seduction to them. In either instance—a generalized white or a multicolored palette—a similar revamping is revealed with a desire to resemble the tourist's stereotyped image. Attaining recognition through one's fantasy of us becomes a common exercise in renunciation and duplicity.

Faced with this phenomenon that seeks to transform the geography of color into a vulgar strategy for communication, the Lenclos offer a progressive rule that combines order and movement. The method described for the village of Viviers in the Ardèche region of France illustrates this practice: begin with the analysis of a site—a global perception or a tendency toward elementary perception—and after the work of taking notes and collecting materials, drawings, and perspectives, end up with a chromatic synthesis that traces both the site's line of permanence (the *basso continuo*) and its line of chromatic specificities. Today, this method of seeing—it is clearly the observer making the landscape—is used in every country where color in national heritage takes on a cultural, social, and economic dimension. May our two travelers never forget, color sticks to the land and refuses to don the tattered robes of ideological discourse. Every country, every village, every city should be familiar with the chromatic genealogy that has designed it, in order to affirm its differences and express, through its skin, an interiority and continuity. We know that geography is another way of studying history. As the Lenclos reveal to us, it is still a history about color, like a person's shifts in pleasure and mood that slowly describe to us their whole being.

THE GEOGRAPHY OF COLOR: A CHROMATIC ITINERARY

Jean-Philippe Lenclos

1/2

OPPOSITE 1/2

To use the words of Josef Albers, it is through "the interaction of colors" that tonal contrasts occur. In some locations, pigmented, saturated colors communicate forcefully and energetically, while in others, where colors are more achromatic, their articulation is more discreet. It was in Japan, in 1961, that I became aware of the geography of color through the overwhelming differences between the chromatic spectrum in the landscapes of northern France, characterized by warm, terra-cotta colors, and in Japan, where Kyoto's chromatic range is dominated by blacks, grays, and whites.

1

2

The idea of the geography of color was revealed to me on an unexpected path. It was conceived in the meeting of two cultures: the culture of my childhood in northern France, and that of my long stay in Japan, a discovery I made at the age of twenty-two.

In my youthful dreams, this mythic country attracted me above all others with the poetry it emitted in its Zen gardens and ancient architecture, and through the mysterious beauty of its calligraphy.

I arrived in Kyoto in 1961 to study architecture. The discovery of a new culture and landscapes, seen under different skies and different lights, was the origin of a profound and decisive visual shock. I sought in particular to steep myself in this universe of colors so new to me, dominated by the terra-cotta gray of the roofs and the darkly toned patina of the wood walls which stood out strongly against the white shojis[1] of traditional homes.

To the chromatic features of architectural language was added calligraphy, where white space surrounds a sign traced in black ink with a brush. Just as in Chinese painting, the white of the paper represents space and intimates the original void, where the smallest ink stroke, whether fluid or sharp, evokes the original breath in movement and in a permanent tension between fullness and emptiness. Calligraphy is even an illustration of the interaction between yin and yang, the two vital, harmonious, and complementary breaths so dear to the Tao, eternally present in Zen philosophy and aesthetics. White and black, positive and negative, fullness and emptiness, balance out and come together in the traced line of the ideogram, at once sign and pictogram. Through the gestural rhythm of the calligrapher, the white and black are the source of all writing and the genesis of all color, as it suggests the whole range of becoming.

1. Shoji: a sliding window of stretched rice paper.

1

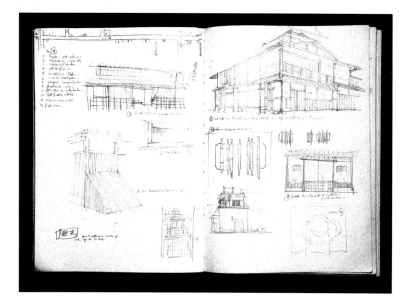

2

3

4

1 / 2 / 3 / 4
Walking through the narrow streets of Kyoto, a sketchpad in hand, I became strikingly aware of a new dimension to color: all colors are based in black and white. Calligraphy, beyond the graphical representation of the brushed sign, demonstrates a perfect balance

and deep interconnectedness between yin and yang, the two complementary breaths that are eternally present in Taoist philosophy and Zen aesthetics. The dialogue between void and presence is perceivable in the black-and-white pictorial language of a Mondrian or Malevitch, a language

that, despite its extreme asceticism, prefigures color.

OPPOSITE 1 / 2 / 3
An attentive eye to landscape and architectural composition reveals the strict complementary natures of fullness and emptiness, rhythm, color,

texture, and material. Color in architecture, just as in painting, is therefore not just an assemblage of tones, as is often believed in the West.

While drawing in the tiny streets of Gion Machi and in gardens and temples, Ryoan-Ji (opposite, 3), Daizen-In Ginkakuji, Kokedera . . . , I was seeing space anew. In the silence, I learned the whole extent of matter and the beauty of rhythms. And the precious shadows of Tanizaki helped me, by pure contrast, to measure the primacy of the light that gave life to every color.

Then the idea came to me, as proof, that Japan's specific colors took part in its cultural identity. This revelation was born of the comparison with my own country of origin, the Pas-de-Calais, in the north of France where Matisse was born—a humid land where the habitat pays tribute to the bright tones of its orange tiles and brick-red facades, contrasting in a Fauvist manner with the intense green of the vegetation.

A

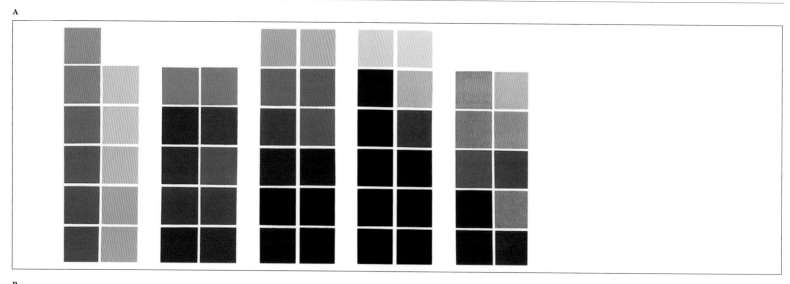

B

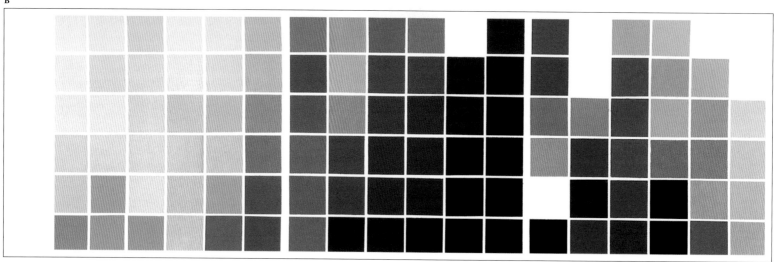

C

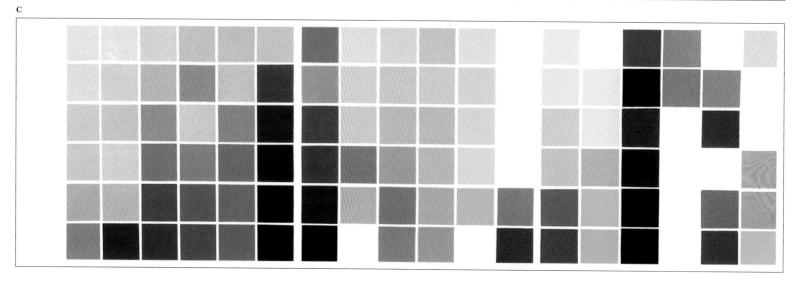

A / B / C
In 1971, the Color Planning Center of Tokyo asked us to perform a first analysis of the city's colors. Three sample charts reveal the dominant chromatics of the architecture: chart **A** assembles colors from traditional exteriors; chart **B** shows the colors in transitional architectures, and chart **C** shows the colors in modern architecture.

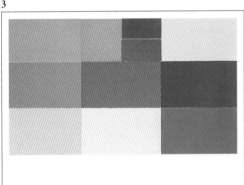

Thus, the concept of the "geography of color" was born in the surprising confrontation between Japan and Pas-de-Calais: each country, each region, each city and village expresses colors that are specific to them. Due to factors as diverse as geography, geological or aquatic environment, or light, to which one may add the socio-cultural behaviors of the inhabitants, these colors determine and contribute to the affirmation of a national, regional, or local identity. This data deserved analysis.

It was in 1965 that our method of analysis began to work itself out little by little, with synthesis charts that allowed for description and emphasis of the chromatic record, as well as a comparison of the results. This comparison spectacularly revealed the specific chromatic character of each country or place.

1 / 2 / 3 / 4
Layout illustrations, made on site with the help of a quick, color-pencil sketch, annotated with the help of color guides, are then divided qualitatively and transposed onto a synthesizing chart (Akasaka Mitsuke, Tokyo, Japan).

1

2

3

4

During the same period, studying a paint color guide intended for the habitat gave me the opportunity to envision a range of colors with respect to architectural tradition and local color. To this end, I initiated a systematic inventory of the colors of the regional habitat in France. The detailed annotations, methodically indexed on site, needed to find a way to communicate. Consequently, our work resulted in the presentation of twenty-five vignettes, in the form of synthesizing color charts, illustrating in detail, yet simply, the colors of each dwelling. This was the point of departure for all of the studies that were subsequently conducted around the world.

The first of these studies was commissioned in 1970 by the Color Planning Center in Tokyo and led to an exhibit at the Ichiban Kan Gallery in Tokyo, in 1972. Japan, which had been precisely the origin of my discovery of the reality of the geography of color, was also the first foreign country where I had the opportunity to develop and publicize my research.

1 / 2 / 3 / 4
During the initial on-site color studies, precise color documentation of the habitat is performed in two different and complementary ways: material sampling, when possible, and color calibration with the help of color guides (1 Karpathos, Greece, 1983; 2 Nagoya, Japan, 1983; 3 Burano, Italy, 1994; 4 Chessy, France, 1989).

1

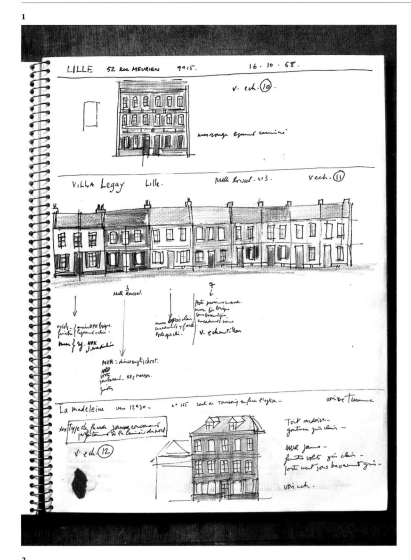

2

4

3

1 / 2 / 3 / 4
Research on the geography of color, originating in the 1960s, is based on the methodical and analytical observation of various visual components that contribute to the individuation of the colored habitat. In fact, this is the most practical tool for clearly delineating the tonalities that make up a design.

(1 Lille, France, 1968; 2 Nagoya, Japan, 1983; 3 Karpathos, Greece, 1983; 4 Burano, Italy, 1987)

1

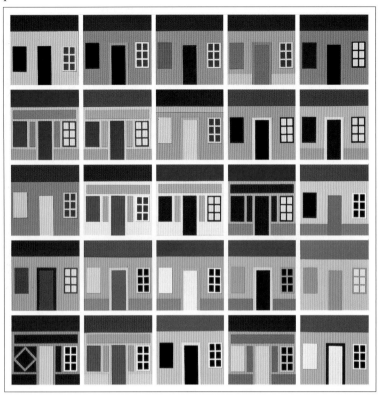

2

3

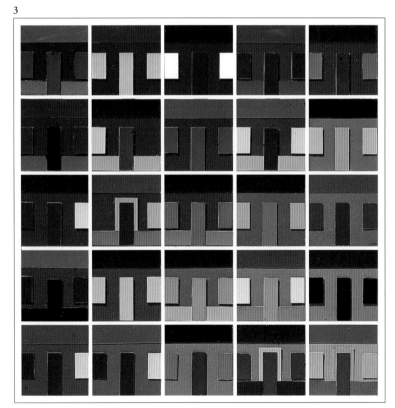

1 / 2 / 3
Our first detailed notations of habitat color were completed in France, starting in 1965. Very quickly, we felt the need to produce the results of our investigations in a synthetic and modular form; this is how we came to the first vignettes that gave details, in a simplified manner, about the details of each habitation. These vignettes were reassembled into charts that synthesized the colors from twenty-five houses. This method of presentation allows for comparisons to be easily drawn between one site and another.

As you can see, these three synthesizing charts, made from various analyses in France, clearly show the chromatic identity for each of the sites in the study (1 Giverny, Ile-de-France; 2 Amboise, Pays de la Loire; 3 Lille region, north).

1

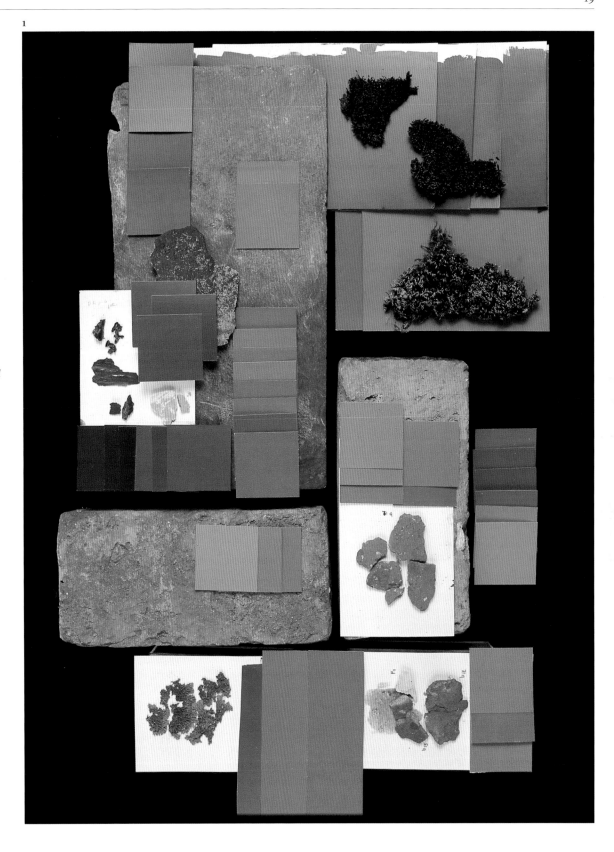

1

Even with drawing and photography as basic methods for collecting the chromatic data of a site or pattern, they cannot take material substance and texture into account. This is why we collect material samples, when possible. These samples act as primary witnesses to the elements of color composition, such as the tactile dimension that is produced by the level of granularity and the various aspects of the material surface (Le Vaudreuil, Normandy).

1

2

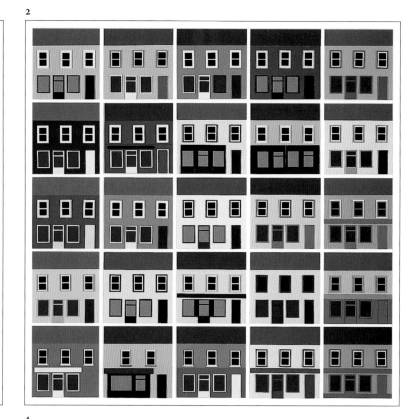

3

4

1/2/3/4
While we began to conduct our research in France in the 1960s, we simultaneously carried out our analytical process in different European countries.

These two pages demonstrate the diversity of local and national chromatic identities, and illustrate the concept of the geography of color as applied to European homes (1 Arkassa, Karpathos, Greece; 2 Kenmare, Ireland; 3 Rättvick, Sweden; 4 Damme, Belgium).

1

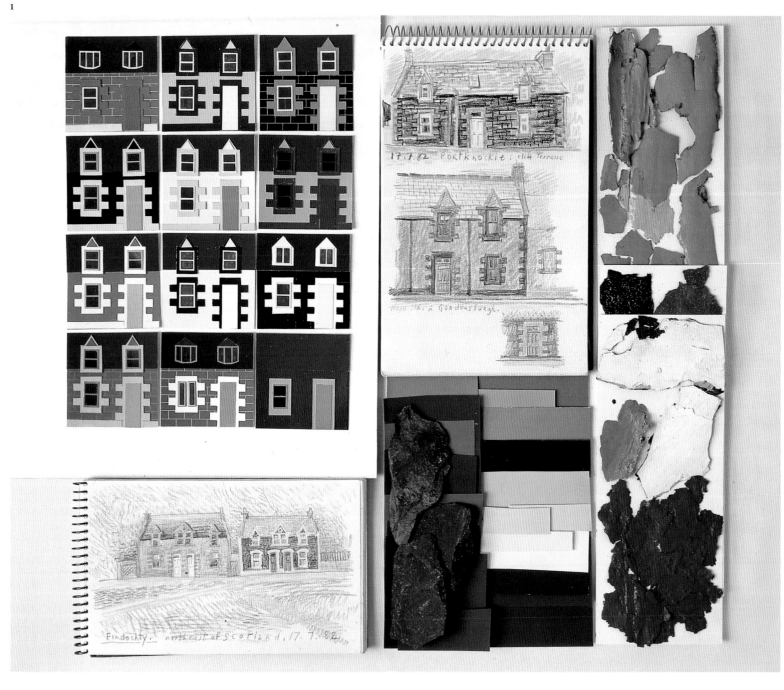

1

This group of documents brings together the various elements that contribute to illustrating the results of our site analysis. Here, we are looking at the northeast of Scotland, with the first notations dating back to 1982. In comparing this synthesizing chart with those that had been made previously, we noticed that each of the vignettes is personalized by the cut of the framework and by the presence of dormers, which are characteristic of architecture in this area of Scotland.

This method of illustration is more narrative and is necessary when an exterior's moldings show a sufficient number of significant idiosyncrasies.

1

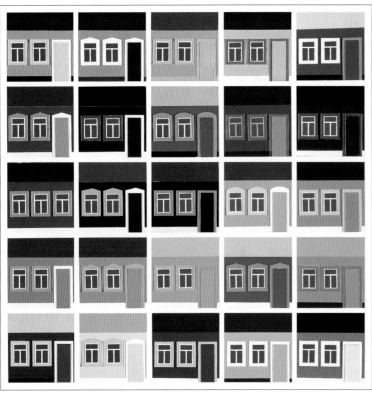

2

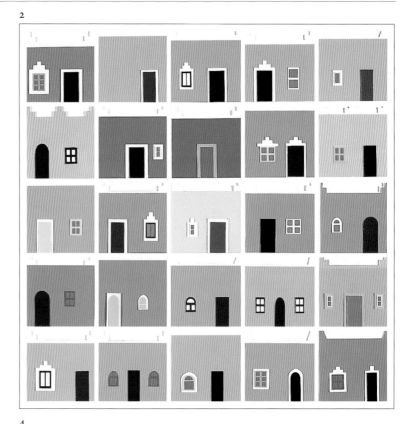

3

4

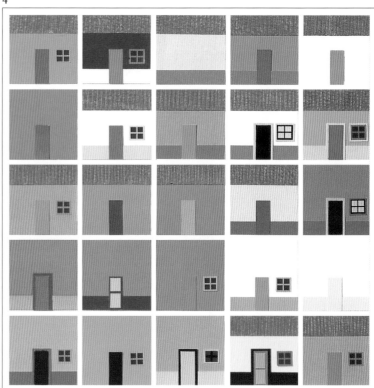

1 / 2 / 3 / 4
Four synthesizing charts, four continents, four color families. These two pages offer an example of the variety of chromatic palettes in popular habitats around the world.

Each of these synthesizing charts expresses either a color dominance or a contrast in tonalities added by a given architecture's moldings, thereby asserting a unique and singular identity.

These visual findings help establish ethnic, social, and cultural data that is closely linked to the geography of color (1 Suzdal, Russia, Europe; 2 Ouarzazate, Morocco, Africa; 3 Jodhpur, India, Asia; 4 Salcaja, Guatemala, Latin America).

1

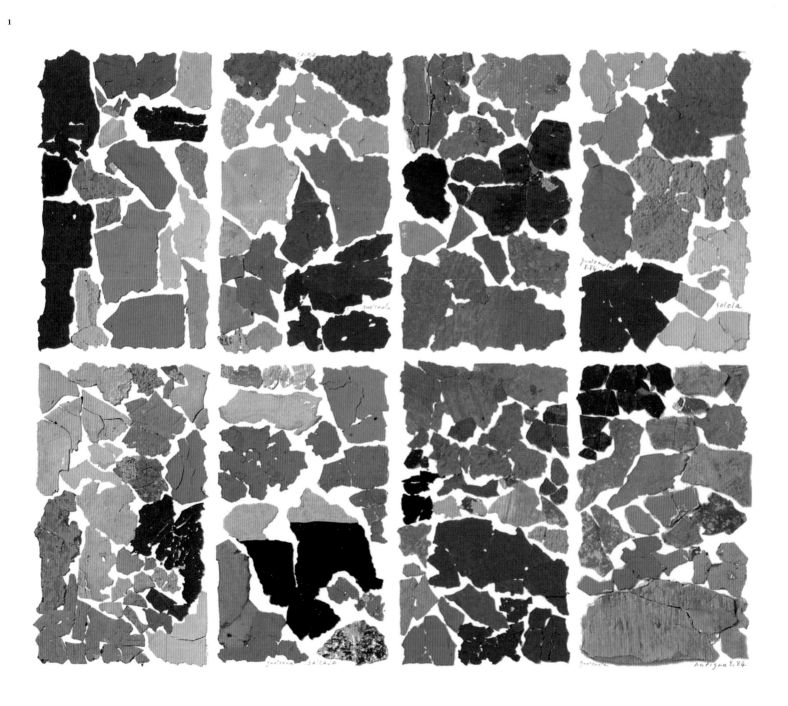

1

Material samples, such as these coatings from our research in Guatemala, offer the most authentic testimony of the color and material that characterize the geography of color of a site or region. You may notice that the tonalities of the synthesizing charts on the facing page are identical to those of the material samples.

COLORS AND SYMBOLS

"Sight immerses us in the symbol through light and darkness, above all through colors," wrote Dominique Zahan in "L'homme et la couleur" (*Histoire des moeurs*), underlining the close relationship between colors and symbols.

This symbolism is universal and can be demonstrated in any domain that touches upon the "human"—religion, morals, and customs, psychology, art, and again, the habitat. The link between color-symbol and religion is obvious. In Mayan culture, for example, the gods gave color to every living thing, and when death made color disappear, there only remained the pallor of bones and cornhusks: "A long time ago, every Mayan knew how to recognize the cycles of life, earth, and the entirety creation, in five symbolic pigments: the red of blood and birth, the yellow of the nourishing corn, the blue-green of water and fertility, the black of death, and the white of mutation. To give meaning to the world, the ancients arranged a map whose center and four cardinal points were associated with these five life-giving colors . . . This cosmic chart determined the orientation of the architecture and its emblem appeared in abundance in painted and sculpted décor."[1] Similarly, for the Chinese, "five primary colors corresponded to the five primary elements, the five directions, and the four seasons: blue (or green), the color of spring and of wood, to the East; red, the color of summer, fire, and heat, to the South; white, the color of autumn and metal, to the West; black, the color of winter and water, to the North; yellow, the color of the Earth and of millet, in the center."[2]

In India, the cult of the goddess Lakshmi, the divinity that protects the home and ensures family health and prosperity, is upheld by women who paint their houses with sacred patterns that have been transmitted from mother to daughter. These images, in different styles according to region, decorate the facade, the doorstep, or simply the doorway through which benevolent and malevolent spirits enter. The holy paintings, applied to a layer of soft clay mixed with cow dung, and achieved with organic pigments—rice flour, natural ochre, henna, and cinnabar, take on an ephemeral characteristic in perfect agreement with the Hindu concept of life in which everything is in transition.

1

1
In Japan, the Country of the Rising Sun, red is the emblematic color for Shinto sanctuaries. The Fushimi Inari Jinja in Kyoto is one of the most famous temples in Japan. Foxes, associated with the protecting divinity of food, and especially rice, are worshipped here. Here you see one of the many planted alleyways of wooden torii (porticos), painted in red, offered by donors and pilgrims.

Originally, these porticos were dedicated to the holy, long-tailed roosters that perched atop to sing to the rising Sun god. According to Shinto religion, the emperor was a descendant of the Sun god, symbolized by the red circle found on the Japanese flag.

1. Jeffrey Becom and Sally Jean Aberg; *Maya Color: The Painted Villages of Mesoamerica*. New York: Abbeville Press, 1997.
2. Song Jian Ming, "Le Codage des couleurs dans l'architecture Chinoise." *Pour la science*, January, 1993.

1

1

In the Madras region of India, women make daily kolam, holy drawings created at their doorstep before sunrise to greet the goddess Lakshmi, the protectress of the home. Starting with a traditional weave composed of thirty-six points, the mother of the family pours the fine rice powder with her fingers, creating ritual patterns that are refreshed daily. Monochromatic during the week, the pattern is enriched with color and complexity on Sundays and holidays (Perungudi, near Madurai).

In South Africa, in the Sotho and Ndebele tribes, mural painting has an equally sacred quality, bearing witness to their faithfulness to tradition. The symbolic colors—the red ochre extracted from the land, the white of limewater, the black of coal— are used in transitional zones in the home, that is to say, along the base and tops of buildings, and around openings. In the catalog for the Courtyard exhibit presented in Paris in 1996, Gary N. Van Wyk, who collects documents on paintings that Basotho women compose on the walls of their homes, explains their ritual importance in the following words: "The links that connect the house, the land, and the women are completely evident during the women's initiation ceremonies, which are still practiced today nearly everywhere. The four steps in the rites of passage are identified by the different earthen colors that coat the women's bodies, each color having its own symbolic significance.

"To begin, the initiates are covered in white soil, which symbolizes the serenity and purity prior to crossing the threshold into adulthood. At the first, subsequent full moon, they wash in the river and are covered in black soil, which is associated with the dark rain clouds sent by their ancestors. During the third stage, they are once again covered in white ochre . . . Patterns similar to those adorning architecture, particularly those that accentuate the entryway, are drawn onto their legs, which have already been coated in white. At this stage of the initiation, the female body is very clearly viewed as a parallel of the home. During the final ceremony, the women are covered in red ochre. Known as *latsoko*, blood of the earth, this color represents menstrual blood, a sign of fertility . . . The red ochre also recalls the water and rain sent by the ancestors . . . "

Likewise, Gary N. Van Wyk draws attention to the use of color in dwelling as a means of political resistance: "Before the arrival of democracy in 1994, the colors of the ANC (African National Congress) burst forth from murals and signified the inhabitants' opposition to the apartheid regime . . . a dangerous act of resistance . . . almost invisible, however, to white observers . . . A home painted yellow and green seemed innocent enough, but when the door was open, the dark interior stuck out like a black rectangle to finish off the flag of the resistance movement."

1

2

1

In several religions, green is the color of resurrection and symbolizes the first level of spiritual regeneration. In Islam, green is the color of the Prophet and recalls the "garden of delights," the Eden promised to believers. In Ghardaia, as elsewhere in M'zab, houses painted in green or turquoise tones indicate that the inhabitants have made the pilgrimage to Mecca (Ghardaia, Algerian Sahara).

2

For the Sotho, the colors and exterior designs of traditional homes have a symbolic character. Red ochre in particular evokes the rain sent by ancestors. Facade designs around openings and in transitional zones, such as along the base or top edge, display the residents' fidelity to tradition (South Africa).

OPPOSITE 1

Blue, green, and blue-green are sacred colors in Iran, evoking paradise, the Garden of Delights, or the City of the Beyond. The dome of the Shah's Mosque, with its large, branching design, recalls the Touba Tree, or Tree of Eternal Happiness, itself a symbol of the paradise promised to believers. The blue, glazed tile designed for the domes of religious buildings was a specialty of the city of Kashan, which lent its name to the enameled brick squares, kashi (the Shah's Mosque, Isfahan).

OPPOSITE 2

From the earliest days of human history, the rainbow has been an object of fascination and it is understandable that, for the ancients, it was interpreted as a sign from the gods. Because of its scale, its immateriality, and its spectral chain of luminous colors arching in geometric perfection through space, the rainbow came to symbolize a type of communication between the other world and the Earth (Saint-Quay-Portrieux, France).

The color *par excellence*—the color among colors—is red. In several languages, red is a synonym for color, beauty, or even wealth.

In Sweden, in the sixteenth century, under the reign of Johan III, red paint was reserved for the privileged classes; it remained a sign of wealth for a long time, so much so that during the revolt that broke out in Dalecarlie in 1743, the insurgent peasants decided to "pillage and bring devastation upon the ruling classes, beginning with the presbyteries and other dwellings painted in red."

Red is, it seems, the most ancient color used by human beings. During the prehistoric era, the dead were covered in red ochre. It may be assumed that our ancestors were expressing some belief in an afterlife. For the Russian orthodox, Easter Sunday, the day of Christ's resurrection, is red, like the triumph of life.

Red is a symbol of life, beauty, and power. In ancient Rome, a variant of red—reddish purple—was the color of supreme power and traders of red fabric were punished by death under the Justinian code. In the Bible, God gave Moses the following instructions regarding the construction of the tabernacle: "The gate of the court shall be composed of a curtain twenty cubits long, of violet-purple, scarlet, and crimson, and of fine twisted linen" (Exod. 27). Red is the color of fire, blood, and action; warriors dressed in red in traditional India and in Iran.

In Guatemala, the Mayan temples were inundated in red paint, the color of the rising sun and of sacrificial blood. At the dawn of creation, the gods offered forth their blood mixed with corn paste in order to create the Mayan people. And, in exchange for red blood, a drink that quenched their thirst, they spread their goodness over the earth in the form of rain, thereby allowing bountiful corn harvests, a staple of the Mayas, from dawn to dusk, from birth to death. For the Christianized Mayas of today, red has become the color of Jesus' blood. In the Far East, red, the color of fire, has the reputation of staving off this scourge; as such it is used in rites of construction.

Red is also the color of the divine Love to which we are led by Dionysius, who is represented as dressed in a red cloak; it is the color of the Holy Spirit, whose tongues of fire descended upon the apostles on the day of the Pentecost; it is a fire of love that inspires, purifies, and regenerates. On the island of Mykonos, in Greece, church and chapel cupolas are red in honor of the Holy Spirit.

1

Red is the color of colors: in many languages, red is synonymous with color and beauty. In traditional habitations, regardless of the country, red was usually obtained from iron oxides. In Sweden, for example, red paint, which was for a long time reserved for the privileged classes, was based on pigments from the Falun mines, hence the name "Falun red." One of the three primary colors, red is often used as the color for signals and emblems; this is undoubtedly what inspired the owners of the Irish bar, Kelly's Korner. Facades in Burano incorporate the colors of the Italian flag: red, white, and green (1 Burano, Italy; 2 Sigtuna, Sweden; 3 Killarney, Ireland; 4 Aspen, United States).

The complementary color to red is green. It is the color of the vegetable realm, of water (as red is the color of fire), of the goddess Aphrodite, born of the sea, a personification of Nature. A reassuring, refreshing, and balancing color, green is the color of hope for Christians; it is the color of the prophets, of Saint John the Evangelist, the Holy Spirit's herald; for Muslims, the green robe of the Prophet became the color of Islam, and the green flag comprised the emblem of salvation and the symbol of all riches, whether material or spiritual. However, in the M'zab, a region of the Algerian Sahara, only the inhabitants who have made the pilgrimage to Mecca are allowed to paint their houses in green and turquoise hues. In every religion, green symbolizes the first degree of spiritual regeneration.

With the triumph of spring over winter, green is the symbol of victory. In Ireland, it is not only the color of Saint Patrick (many homes are painted green in honor of the patron saint), but is also the color of defiance worn by the Irish to affirm their independence and freedom from the English. Since the 1980s, green has been the symbolic color of environmental defense movements.

However, green is also the color of mildew and decay, which is strange. For a long time, this unstable color has been very closely tied to the idea of change, fate, chance, and destiny. The various symbolic aspects of the color green, seemingly contradictory, coexist in the Muslim world: "For the inhabitants of the sweltering countries of Arabia and the regions of the Middle East, greenery represents beneficent shading, the coolness we desire, the presence of water, wealth and happiness. Green, therefore, symbolizes Eden. It is the color of Paradise, and similarly the color of its Prophet. Often, in Islamic countries, the custom is to have an intensely green flag waving over the tombs of marabouts and over the mausoleums of venerated holy persons."[1] Henri Stierlin develops his idea: "Furthermore, the association between the color green and death comes from an antiquity beyond the reaches of memory: green is the color of resurrection, because it characterizes spring which is itself a rebirth of nature."

1 / 2 / 3 / 4
Green is a secondary color obtained by mixing blue and yellow, and the complementary color to red. This color evokes water and vegetation and was adopted by ecologists at the end of the 1980s as a symbol of their fight against all forms of pollution. For the Mayas, blue-green is associated with everything that was precious: rain, the young corn buds, jade, and quetzal feathers. Green is the emblematic color of Ireland with its vast and verdant prairies; it is one of the colors on the national flag and the color of Saint Patrick, Ireland's patron saint. The range of different green tones is the most extensive: in antiquity, there was already a distinction between leek green, apple green, olive green, and toad green (1 Dinkelsbühl, Germany; 2 Salcaja, Guatemala; 3 San Francisco, United States; 4 Toormore, Ireland).

1. Henri Stierlin, *Isfahan: image du paradis*. Geneva: Sigma, 1976.

If green is the color of water, blue is the color of air and sky and of all that is far away. It is the deepest and most immaterial of colors, but also the coldest and, along with white, the most pure. It is therefore the sign of the Virgin, and in certain regions of Poland, it was traditional to paint the houses of eligible young women in blue. The small town of Weyersheim, in Alsace, still preserves a couple of older homes painted in a bluewash, witnesses to an era when the inhabitants rigorously confirmed their affiliation to the Catholic church in a Protestant environment.

Blue is also the symbol of divine wisdom, of the Holy Spirit, the spirit of wisdom and truth, and of *Vairocana*, the transcendent Wisdom of Tibetan Buddhism. Likewise, in Iran, the colors blue and blue-green have a talismanic quality. On glazed ceramic tiles, very early on, these colors covered architectural surfaces designed to decorate religious buildings.

For the Mayas, blue-green was the preeminent holy color, and, on a larger scale, it was associated with everything that was precious for them: the fertile rain, the young buds of corn, jade, and quetzal feathers which were sometimes blue, sometimes green. "In ancient times, blue-green was the mark of priests, royalty, and offerings to the gods. Sacrificial victims were consecrated with blue pitch, as were the temple stairs they climbed and the stone on which they were skinned alive. In the course of the Mayan month of Yax, in the middle of winter, all valued objects—fishing nets that hung in entryways, for example—were anointed with blue-green paint. Nevertheless, blue and green were applied sparingly on the great pyramids because of the scarcity of the pigments. A short time before the conquest of Maya, prophecies and dark premonitions left the people little hope. It was only then, in desperation, that the cities—such as Tulum and Mayapan—threatened with attack, could procure enough blue pigment in order to cover their walls with its regenerative powers."[1]

1 / 2 / 3 / 4
Like red and yellow, blue is one of the three primary colors. Statistically, it is the favored color of Europeans. Blue is the color of the air and sky. In the Catholic religion, it is associated with the Virgin Mary and in Alsace, for example, Catholics paint their homes blue to distinguish themselves from neighboring Protestant houses, which were often red. More generally, blue is a symbol of divine wisdom and is the color of souls and spirituality (1 *Châtenois, Alsace, France;* 2 *Bornholm Island, Denmark;* 3 *Aspen, United States;* 4 *Gravata, Brazil*).

Today, blue is the color of large international institutes, in light of its neutral and pacific qualities. Surveys show that it is by far the favored color of the Western world, except among the Spanish. This evolution began in the thirteenth century and is therefore not a new phenomenon.

1. Jeffrey Becom and Sally Jean Aberg, *Maya Color: The Painted Villages of Mesoamerica*. New York: Abbeville Press, 1997.

Yellow is the warmest and most ardent of colors, like the sun at its zenith, the Golden Light, the path of communication between men and gods. Of divine essence, golden yellow on Earth is characteristic of the powers of princes, kings, and emperors, who thereby proclaim the divine origin of their power. The Chinese bestowed a predominance upon yellow that exists nowhere else. It was the color of emperors during the Ming dynasty, then in the Qing dynasty, both in their clothing and on the tiles that adorned the imperial palaces. Green was reserved for the homes of the nobility; blue for sanctuaries, like the Temple of the Sky in Beijing; and matte black or gray was reserved for other edifices. The color yellow, which symbolized the Earth, and by extension, Chinese territory, the Emperor, and the Son of the Sky, demonstrated that he was the center of the universe. In ancient Greece, religious orders imposed yellow for the marital veil and for the tunics of young girls dedicated to Artemis Brauronia (Brauron being, in Attica, the place of worship for the cult of Artemis of Tauride). Toward the end of Roman antiquity, yellow was similarly a very sought after color, a holy color. In contrast, in India, yellow is the color of undyed fabrics, appropriate to the Vaisya caste, or farmers, whose clothing turned earthen in color as it became dirty, whereas white belonged to the Brahman and red to the warrior.

Yellow is also the color of adulterous men, and by extension, the color of the betrayed husband and of the traitor. Michel Pastoreau notes that in medieval iconography, Judas is often dressed either totally or partially in yellow. We have noticed, for example, that in the frescos of the Saint-Gomery Chapel in Brittany, in the Côtes-d'Armor region, Judas is distinct from the other apostles in his completely yellow dress. In the fourteenth century, disloyal knights had the door of their home smeared with yellow; this custom was used against the army commander of Bourbon.

1 / 2 / 3 / 4
After red and blue, yellow is the third primary color. It is the lightest of all of the spectrum's colors and the most luminous as well, since it has the most reflective ability. It is the symbol of life, wealth, and light. The Chinese gave yellow a prevalence not seen anywhere else: it was the color of the Emperor, both for his clothes and for the tiles that covered his palace. In dwellings, blue is often the secondary color that accompanies yellow (1 Condado, Brazil; 2 Bornholm Island, Denmark; 3 Alcantariha, Portugal; 4 Suzdal, Russia).

White is the sum of all colors of the spectrum, thus it is the sum of all radiant colors. As the most luminous color, white symbolizes purity, virginity, and innocence. First Communicants and young brides are fully dressed in white; it is the color of the pope, of priests, and of certain religious orders, and already in the time of the Celts, it was the color reserved for druids.

White is the color of initiation. In sub-Saharan Africa, initiates are sometimes painted with a white plaster to mark the beginning of their spiritual life; in Catholicism, during the baptismal ceremony, the baptized are dressed in white clothing to mark the start of a new life and to symbolize their entrance into the larger family of the children of God. During the Spanish conquest of Mayan territory, the red on the places of worship, associated in the conquerors' minds with sin, was replaced with the white of lime milk, a symbol of Catholic purity. It just so happened that white, for the Mayas, was the color of change.

White is the color of revelation and of the transfiguration of Jesus before his apostles: "He was transfigured before them and his clothes became dazzling white, such as no one on Earth could bleach them" (Mk. 9). The Sufi confer great importance on white, symbol of wisdom, and on its relationship to red, symbol of man as prisoner of the world. In Tibetan Buddhism, the Dalai Lama is also the Ocean of Wisdom, or even the Lord of the White Lotus. White is also the color of the aristocracy: the color of the king and of the royalist party in France and the color of Brahmans in India. Finally, white is associated with death, and often stands as a sign of mourning, just as black does. The tradition of wrapping the dead in white shrouds dates back to the Egyptians. In China, just as in India, the true color of mourning is white, and likewise in the French court, mourning was carried out in white. The orthodox theologian Olivier Clément explains the symbolism of the white of Holy Saturday in the following terms: "God has died and a hush falls over the earth . . . Christ descends into Hell. This descent is a triumphant one. Christ has come to destroy the blanket of darkness that has weighed down humanity." White is therefore the sign of waiting, the sign of hope. Similarly, Olivier Messiaen, who sought to execute his work *Et Expecto Resurrectionem Mortuorum* on the mountaintop across from the Meije glacier in La Grave, envisions white as follows: "There, through the play of sunlight on the white of the glacier, I will visually obtain the second symbol that circulates through my music, the main quality of the Glorious Body, the gift of clarity . . . "[1]

1/2/3/4
White is the sum of all colors. In 1676, Newton was the first to dissect a beam of white light with the help of a triangular prism, obtaining the colors of the spectrum, which are all the colors of the rainbow. White, like black, is said to be an achromatic tone.

White is the color of initiation, revelation, purity, and wisdom. For habitations, white is the symbol of cleanliness and hygiene. In numerous countries, especially around the Mediterranean, purifying and protecting limewater is generally washed onto the walls of the dwelling, and even on its doorstep (1 Shibam, Yemen; 2 Concarneau, France; 3 Bornholm Island, Denmark; 4 Casares, Spain).

1. Olivier Messiaen, *Musique et couleur.* Paris: P. Belfond, 1986.

Black is both white's equal and opposite; like white, it is situated at the two extremities of the chromatic spectrum. The duality of black and white is also that like of shadow and light, night and day, sky and earth, purity and uncleanness, and yin and yang. Genesis and various other cosmogonies tell of light's combat against darkness.

As with white, black is a color of mourning, but of a mourning without hope: "Like an oblivion without possibility, like a dead void after the sun's death, like an eternal silence, without future, without even the hope of a future, black resonates internally," writes Wassily Kandinsky in *On the Spiritual in Art*.

Black is the color for mourning in ancient Greece, in Iran and in Islam. In Western Europe, it appears that the association between black and mourning is a relatively recent development and that, at first, it was simply a question of avoiding wearing noticeably colored clothes.

Today however, in France, black and mourning are no longer synonymous, at least in terms of clothing: artists and young people often dress completely in black and who is the woman who doesn't have the obligatory "little black dress" in her closet? In terms of habitats on the other hand, the French continue to exhibit much reticence over using black paint, even in carpentry, whereas in England, Scotland, and Holland, it is a color that plays an integral role in the chromatic palette of walls and detailing work.

Black was the color of vestment style in Italy beginning in the fourteenth century, following the promulgation of economic laws forbidding the use of expensive colorants. All over Europe, the use of black spread, above all in princely courts. The Reformation reaffirmed this propensity by declaring warm colors immoral and by favoring predominantly strict and austere colors.

As for the rainbow, which brings together all the color of the spectrum, it establishes a divine tie between men on one side, and gods or heroes on the other. It is the staircase of the seven colors that Buddha uses to come back down from heaven; in Greece, it is the color of the scarf of the goddess Iris that carries Zeus's decisions to the other gods or to the mere mortals; in China, the sign of the union between yin and yang; for the Hebrews, the materialization of the covenant between God and his people: "And God said: This is the sign of the covenant that I make between me and you and every living creature among you, for all future generations: I have set my bow in the clouds, and it shall be a sign of the covenant between me and the Earth" (Gn. 9, 12, 17).

Black is the preeminent achromatic color, since there is no true black without depriving a space of light. This is undoubtedly why black has been assigned negative values: evil, death, the devil. Still, this color, or rather non-color, is not always associated with such dark symbols; it is sometimes synonymous with asceticism and austerity, in religious clothing for example. In architecture, it is not uncommon to find homes in Protestant countries painted black, which you wouldn't find in predominantly Catholic countries (1 Sotho dwelling, South Africa; 2 Aspen, United States; 3 Findochty, Scotland; 4 San Francisco, United States).

CONSTRUCTION MATERIALS

Whereas in France and in most European countries stone and brick traditionally have been the most commonly used building materials and the notion of a solid dwelling prevailed, it was not the same on other continents where soil and vegetation remain the most widely used base materials, despite a move toward cinder block construction. As a result, we will spend more time in this text on the practical and aesthetic characteristics of earth and wood than on those of stone and brick, already largely developed in *Colors of France* and *Colors of Europe.*

1

In traditional societies, the choice of construction style is a reflection of various factors: climate, the availability of local and nearby resources, technical ability, aesthetic sensibilities, respect for social and religious tradition, and the mobility of the inhabitants, etc.

In the same situation, there are often different, suitable solutions. Why does one prevail over the other? It's a bit of a mystery; this is where we choose to exercise our freedom and creativity.

If we compare earth and wood to stone and brick, we notice that the former are living materials that evolve under climatic influence and therefore require continuous maintenance to prevent deterioration, collapse, or a return to their natural state. On a chromatic level, in their rough state these materials are favorable to a perfect integration of dwelling and environment, and when they are covered in a protective wash or paint, often serve as frequently renovated décor, allowing for total freedom of the inhabitants' creative genius, whether they live in an adobe in Lesotho or a San Francisco "Painted Lady."

1/2/3

OPPOSITE 1
Since antiquity, thatching, a plant-based covering, has been utilized across every continent in every shape and form. Depending on the country and local tradition, its use comes in numerous variations.

Colors and materials are inseparable here and give the dwelling a warm character that recalls the softness of animal pelts (1 Looport, South Africa; 2 Khuri, Rajasthan, India; 3 Normandy, France; opposite, 1 Khuri, Rajasthan, India).

1

VEGETATION

This constitutes the primary available and plentiful material on site. Depending on the country and region, builders have used bamboo, palmyra and millet stalks, coconut and palm leaves, vines, rush, and reeds. These elements, along with certain tree branches and barks, factor into the construction of a dwelling's roof, partitions, and fencing. In Niger, for example, huts made of secco, a switch grass with a long, resistant stalk, are very common in the countryside because of its modest price and insulating qualities; there are also palm-leaf huts near date palm plantations.

For roofing, straw is an ideal covering material that is easily found on site. The straw is tied, then stacked and layered starting from the lower edge of the roof up to the peak; the straw beams are then attached to the frame. This work requires few tools and can be performed by men and women alike.

Bamboo is a treelike grass found in humid tropical areas that grows extremely rapidly and can reach up to 66 feet (20 meters) in height. It supplies a construction material that is much appreciated for its numerous qualities: exceptionally supple, bamboo can support heavy weight without breaking; hollow, it is quite light; moreover, it is practically immune to change in atmospheric conditions. Its use is quite common in Far East construction. In Japan, there are around one hundred varieties of bamboo, each one corresponding to a particular use; the madake family is the most utilized. In Cameroon for example, this plant is regularly used for craftwork, agriculture, furniture production, and home construction. "In construction, split bamboo serves as an armor for earthen walls, fencing, and hedges around dwellings, notably in cities (the bamboo walls in Douala, China), and as a frame surrounding round, square, and rectangular houses." Mohaman Haman, in his work on "bamboo and the capabilities of local initiatives in Cameroon," explains further: "Bamboo constructions have always been a part of building heritage in southern and western Cameroon. Associated with vegetation and soil, it naturally presented itself and has remained the dominant technology in villages and chiefdoms up until the years of independence." After having been a bit forgotten and left aside, traditional construction techniques based on locally available materials are being rediscovered by local authorities and supported by organizations. In this way, the sultan Njoya, a Bamun king, sought to reconstruct the former palace of the Bamun kings at Koutaba in western Cameroon following traditional building methods.

2

3

4

1

1

OPPOSITE 1 / 2 / 3 / 4
These two pages show a couple of examples of the use of bamboo and wood in traditional architecture. In Russia, log houses are part of the everyday landscape in a country where winters are long and rigorous;

untreated wood develops a gray patina over time, colored in soft and lively shades. In the Far East, there are hundreds of bamboo varieties, each one corresponding to a specific use; the superior quality of the material and its lanky character lend themselves to delicate pattern compositions.

Bamboo, often integrated with wood and thatching, helps to create chromatic ensembles with related tones and values (1 Suzdal, Russia; opposite, 1 Nasushiobara, Japan; 2 Kyoto, Japan; 3 Anhui Province, China; 4 Murotsu, Japan).

OPPOSITE 1/2/3
Wood was long considered the most practical and economic construction material, especially in places that lacked stone. Today it is still utilized in many countries as the sole base material, a building framework, or as a covering for exteriors. It is often left natural, but is most often protected with permeating varnish or paint, as is the case in Russia and Nordic countries. The Katsura villa, built in the seventeenth century near Kyoto, was the summer residence of the emperor's brother. Its architecture, which is extremely sober, is widely regarded as the archetype for modular construction that inspired twentieth-century artists such as Mies van der Rohe (1 Porvoo, Finland; opposite, 1 Marken, Netherlands; 2 Dinkelsbühl, Germany; 3 Katsura villa, Kyoto, Japan).

WOOD

In European countries, wood was long considered the most practical and economical building material. Additionally, it offered the advantage of being reusable from one construction to the next. Whole cities were built of wood; this was notably the case in London where wood was ultimately replaced by brick and stone because of fires. In northern Europe, entire cities disappeared in flames without leaving a trace. However, certain older buildings have survived, like the stave churches of Norway, built in the eleventh and twelfth centuries by shipbuilders. Still today, in countries with harsh winters, like in Russia and Scandinavia, a large number of rural and even city dwellings have remained faithful to traditional materials, because of the need to retain heat.

The European tradition of constructing with wood won over North America and is solidly ensconced in the United States and Canada.

However, Europe is not home to the most ancient buildings made of wood; that is in Nara, Japan, where the Buddhist temple of Horyu-Ji, with its five-story pagoda, was built in the seventh century! In China, the Shijia pagoda, which dates back to the eleventh century, reaches one 197 feet (60 meters) high. Also in Asia, the Katsura villa in Kyoto offers one of the most remarkable examples of wood architecture in the world. Furthermore, in Japan, wood was the only construction material up until the Meiji period because it was abundant, easy to find, and particularly well adapted to the country's climate.

Since the beginning of time, and in every region of the world, man has used wood, whether alone, according to a technique of assembling boards that overlap each other or according to the primitive process of stacking logs, or in combination with other materials utilizing framing techniques which date back to the stone age. With half-timber construction, an innovative combination of earth and wood was born, the former being fire resistant, the latter protecting the whole structure against rain.

This type of construction is commonly used around the world, the filling of the structure completed with whatever the builder has on hand: soil, straw, stone, brick, animal manure, etc. When the partitions are not entirely painted over, the overall half-timber construction exhibits markedly different decorative structures from one country to the next.[1]

The frame is sometimes protected—above all on walls that are exposed to rain—by large wooden coverings, such as friezes (planks arranged vertically), covering joints (planks arranged horizontally or at an angle), and shingles (slices of wood arranged like slate roofing).

1. Jean-Philippe and Dominique Lenclos, *Couleurs de L'Europe*. Paris: Editions du Moniteur, 1995.

The color and texture of wood depends on the type of tree, the context in which it develops, and the treatments it has undergone. There are no less than thirty thousand different types of wood, among which we make a distinction between hardwood and softwood. Among hardwoods, oak, which is quite resistant, has a color that varies according to species (of which there are about sixty); as for chestnut, which is also very durable, it exhibits bluish-yellow and light yellow tones.

The most widely used softwoods include spruce, a lightly shimmering white wood; fir, which is very resistant and matte white with a slightly reddish core; and larch, comparable in quality to fir, but exhibiting a finer, narrower grain and a red-salmon tinge with dark veins.

Traditional Japanese construction relies principally on cedar, pine, cypress, and fir; hinoki, a very finely grained blond cypress, is specifically reserved for temples and the most refined homes.

Among tropical hardwoods, numerous species are used in building, for the frame, the walls, and the exterior carpentry. The chocolate-brown azobe, the yellowish-brown iroko, the pinkish-brown makore, the yellow and rosy-brown movingui, the red-brown or rosy-brown niangon, the rosy-brown sapelli, and the reddish-brown sipo with its violet glints are all indigenous to Africa, while the reddish-brown meranti or "dark red" and the Mengkuland, whose tones range from light pink to reddish brown, come from Southeast Asia.

1

2

3

SOIL

Along with wood, soil shares the honor of being one of the most ancient building materials used by man for his dwelling. After being used to fill in the cracks in the first wood homes, it became a building material in its own right as soon as wood became scarce due to rapid deforestation. With or without wooden supports, raw clay construction dates back to the most ancient times. If wood was a natural choice in locations where it was abundant, it was clay soil that lent itself easily to the fabrication of human shelter in any part of the world with a dry climate. It was here that earthen architecture originated, allowing for places such as the Chaldean and Assyrian palaces to be achieved. Many countries as diverse as Saharan Sudan, southern Morocco, Egypt, Iran, and northern China have drawn this easily manipulated and multifaceted material directly from their land.

Today, this material remains widespread in almost all of Africa, the Middle East, and Latin America. In sub-Saharan Africa, where clay earth abounds, "the soil is taken on site or from along waterways and swamps. Termite colonies are equally coveted. Full of sticky substances secreted by the insects, it serves as a bonding agent and helps in the hardening process," explains Manuel Valentin.[1] In Europe as well, earth was a widely used material even in regions where the climate was unfavorable. The great enemy of earth is water, which, through floods and heavy downpours, melts walls. There are earthen buildings in Sweden, Denmark, Germany, in Eastern countries, England, and France.

COLORS OF THE EARTH

In its pure form, clay, consisting essentially of hydrated silicates of aluminum, is white, but it tends to be mixed with various substances that change its physical properties. These impurities (iron oxide, manganese, copper, etc.) create the green, blue, gray, yellow, red, and brown colors.

There is a distinction made between "ochres"—colored yellow, red, or an intermediary hue—and brown, green, or black "earth" colors. In Europe, colorants continue to be extracted from the land: in France (particularly ochre in the Vaucluse region and sienna in the Ardennes), in Italy (mainly in the Veneto, where there are beds of green, red, yellow, and black earth), and in Cyprus, where ochre, green earth, and raw umber form. Competition from synthetic pigments and colorants along with insufficient removal methods has led to the closing of several quarries across Europe.

1

1. In *De terre, de paille et de bois: symbolique de l'architecture en Afrique noire*. Paris: Musée de l'Homme, 1998.

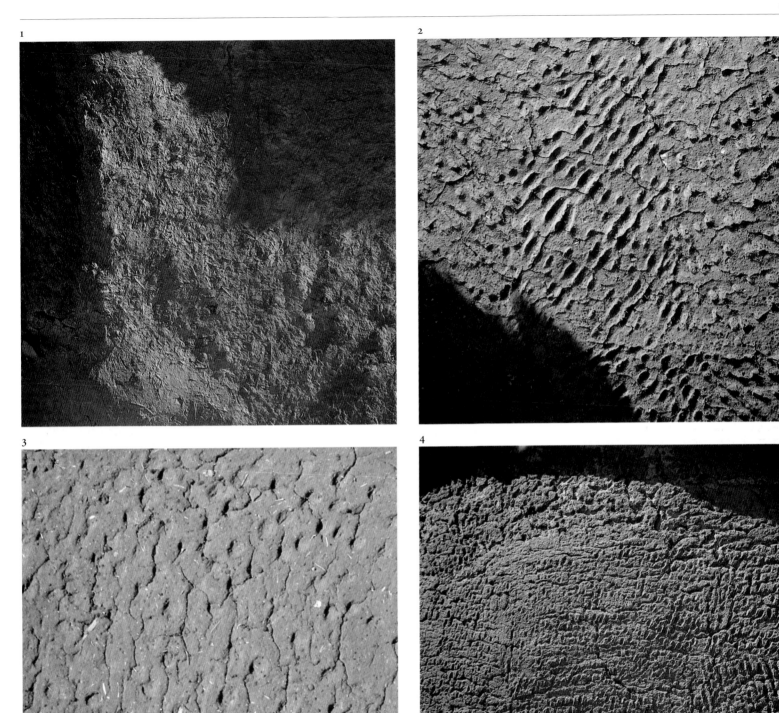

1 / 2 / 3 / 4

OPPOSITE 1

Across Africa, soil is widely used as a construction material. From the modest huts of Lesotho and South Africa to the imposing kasbahs of southern Morocco, adobe construction not only lends itself to a wide variety of architectural forms, but also shows a range of local earthen colors and textures, shaped according to ancestral tradition (1 Dra Valley, Morocco; 2 / 3 / 4 Lesotho, South Africa; opposite, 1 Dra Valley, Morocco).

CONSTRUCTION TECHNIQUES

One of the characteristics of earthen construction is the large variety of techniques utilized. We will not touch upon baked clay, which allows for the production of roof tiles and bricks for walls, as it is not a dominant material in the parts of the world that are the subject of this study.

Pisé, or adobe, construction is a process in which the soil of the site is put to use without relying on straw, filler, or any piece of wood. Adobe is obtained by mixing soil with slightly moist sand that has been compacted with a pestle, or *pisoir*, within a casing called a *banche*. Each filled and compacted banche becomes a piece of wall 16 to 20 inches (40 to 50 centimeters) wide and 10 feet (3 meters) long. These adobe constructions are found in countries as diverse as Morocco, Peru, China, and Scandinavian countries. In France, in the regions of Brittany, Auvergne, and Dauphiné, a large number of homes incorporate compacted soil. With proper plastering, these houses can last several centuries.

In southern Morocco, earthen architecture is used in the building of imposing kasbahs that house entire families, or even ksours, veritable villages surrounded by red-ochre adobe walls. An economic and insulating material, adobe has remarkable visual qualities—the earthen texture discernible even through plaster or whitewashing—structural qualities, due to the putlock holes, more or less filled in, that animate the wall surface, and, when left unpainted, a certain quality of coloration, with warm tones ranging from yellow to orangey-brown depending on where the clay is extracted.

When it is not plastered, cob offers the same chromatic quality as adobe as well as a comparable material richness. Cob is often slightly different because of the mix of the clay and fibrous materials such as cut straw, hay, or heather. While adobe is used in the construction of bearing walls, cob is used for filling in the intervals between wood sections in half-timber homes.

Another technique consists of modeling the soil directly, without mold, casing, or wooden supports. In sub-Saharan Africa and Yemen, there are remarkable examples of shaping which involve knowledge of the earthen material and an enviable know-how.

In North Yemen, in the eastern and northeastern sections of the country, earthen architecture reaches surprising heights with the help of a unique technique that consists of overlaying large tubes of mud mixed with clay soil, sand, and straw, and moistened with water, which is then stomped upon until a certain uniformity is attained. The flat roof is plastered with a salt- and lime-based mortar.

In France, the "bourrines" of the Breton swamps give another example of directly shaping the soil: they are made of *bauge*, soil blended with the straw of chopped reeds. Because of their fragility, the lime-whitened walls are low and quite thick and openings are few, but once completed, this type of house manages well in windy winters. This type of construction is also found in Great Britain, in entire villages in Scotland and Devon.

As for adobe, a crude clay brick, known to this day as *banco*, has been used as material for millennia. The soil blended and mixed with plant fibers is still shaped by hand in certain countries in sub-Saharan Africa, such as Togo; elsewhere, it is usually formed in rectangular molds. The resulting bricks are dried in the sun for several days, and then assembled with wet clay.

In sub-Saharan Africa, "banco is the base material for many buildings. It is a mix of clay soil, sand, gravel, and dry grasses, which, depending on the nature of the soil, produces hues ranging from gray-beige to brown ochre. It is applied by hand. Banco is often reinforced with an internal trellis of interlaced branches that are completely covered. The term *poto-poto* refers to the wet soil from which clumps are hand-shaped and often applied to woven, bamboo, and wood structures . . . "[1]

In the Hausa huts of Niger, wood framing can be found on the interior of earthen dwellings, or even on the exterior of shaped banco, which guarantees better protection against rain, thanks to the overhanging roof. In regions that are rich in stone, masonry combines earth and stone to various degrees.

In South Yemen, the most spectacular realizations of clay brick construction can be seen. In cities, the houses climb several stories, and Shibam, especially, inspires admiration and surprise: in the heart of the desert, it rises up with its five hundred raw-clay skyscrapers behind ramparts pierced by a single doorway. The smooth appearance of the tall surfaces that are partially painted white gives the architecture a heavenly air against the backdrop of an intense blue sky.

1. Manuel Valentin, in *De terre, de paille et de bois: symbolique de l'architecture en Afrique noire*. Paris: Musée de l'Homme, 1998.

1

1

OPPOSITE 1 / 2 / 3
Iron oxide creates the main pigment in clay and expresses a wide range of mineral tones: yellow ochre, red ochre, beige, or various sand tones. Light adds its own essential touch to these tones, highlighting relief, substance, *and texture, which are tied to the masonry techniques used. Depending on the time of day, the same material can take on multiple tactile and chromatic characteristics (1 Free State, South Africa; opposite, 1 Sendai, Japan; 2 / 3 Hadramaout Valley, Yemen).*

TODAY

Soil-based building materials are on the road to disappearing nowadays in favor of other, more resistant materials that, little by little, are modifying not only the chromatic characteristics of buildings, but also the architectural structure. The construction of earthen buildings that was previously cost-effective in European countries, insofar as proprietors completed the work themselves, is proving to be taxing for reasons of manpower and unsuitable techniques. What's more, for Latin American and Asian and African countries, the most practical and least expensive material is now a symbol of technological back-wardness and poverty; today social advancement requires cement and concrete. We have noted in the course of our travels in India, Brazil, South Africa and elsewhere, that the inhabitants of modest villages are surprised, and often stunned, that we are interested in their humble abodes. They are not proud of them and, in certain cases, they are ashamed and show us with an elegant gesture the modern cement slab homes they would love to inhabit.

Nevertheless, unique experiments in earthen constructions are being led throughout the world. These include, in France, the new village of adobe homes in l'Isle d'Abeau, near Lyon; in western Algeria, the farming village Mostefa Ben-Brahim, realized by the Ministry of Agriculture's national construction initiatives; in southern Morocco, at Ouarzazate, the construction of vaulted homes, as part of official project for affordable rural housing. In New Mexico, under the influence of intellectual trends, construction with dried clay bricks has for the past twenty years seen a resurgence in a style of traditional architecture originating in the eighteenth and nineteenth centuries that synthesizes Spanish and Indian architecture.

In Egypt, the architect Hassan Fathy consistently looked for ways to use ancient building techniques based on raw clay by adapting them to the modern era and applying the most advanced scientific knowledge. He recalled the story of using this material, its attributes, the problems it posed, and the current solutions: "In arid and dry zones where soil is the only material, erecting brick walls is easy. Nature itself proposed this material to man, when after the harvest, the soil cracked under dry conditions, whereas the mixture of soil and straw formed compact and durable blocks. Crude brick can endure the compressing effect to which it is exposed in the building of rural homes . . . Brick is a living material, which never completely stabilizes and remains sensitive to changes in relative humidity. That is why architects hesitate to use it. Water and humidity are the greatest enemies of raw brick. Soil mechanics has resolved the problem by using stabilizers, bituminous emulsions, paraffin, or wet cement to treat exterior surfaces in order to protect structures against rain and condensation. Asphalt is similarly used so that stem foundations prevent the humidity from resurfacing by capillarity . . . If the rural people knew how to erect walls, they generally failed when faced with the problem of roofing, which must be achieved with materials that are resistant to flexion and tension, whether with wood which is not always available, or with modern materials like steel and reinforced concrete which are available at an elevated cost."[1]

1. In *AA, l'Architecture d'aujourd'hui*, February, 1978.

1 / 2 / 3 / 4
OPPOSITE 1
Brick is the preeminent modular material; in use on every continent since early antiquity, it is essentially raw clay baked by the sun. In countries lacking wood and stone, adobe is still widely used. As the brick bakes, its color varies with soil composition and baking method.

Builders have always known how to play with brick color to highlight moldings and create decorative effects. In addition, brick walls are often entirely whitewashed, or even lacquered, modifying the original color (1 Venice, Italy; 2 South Yemen; 3 Shanghai, China; 4 Montreal, Canada; opposite, 1 New York, United States).

1

2

3

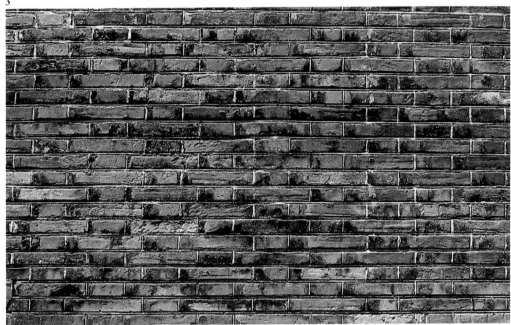

4

We should also point out the restoration projects of these ancient earthen villages. In 1995, when we were in to southern Morocco, the kasbah at Aït ben Haddou, a few miles from Ouarzazate, was undergoing restoration. This remarkable ensemble was restored with local soil and according to traditional methods, while the inhabitants were temporarily housed not far from the village in provisional buildings.

1

OPPOSITE 1 / 2
Color and texture are inseparable. In fact, the same colors and materials change character depending on their surface treatment and finish. In the same way, stone, when it is rough, maintains a structured character and a relief that play off lighting; when it is polished, it takes on a satin, matte, or shiny quality, its color becoming more uniform. Coating the different structural materials underscores the tactile dimension of color (1 Hangzhou, China; opposite, 1 Povoa de Varzim, Portugal; 2 Lesotho, South Africa).

2
In wooden architecture, as is the case in Japan, the same material can take on various characteristics depending on its use and treatment. The color is always practically the same, but its shades vary with shadow and light (2 Murotsu, Japan).

1

2

COATING

Earthen houses are not all covered with a coating. In fact, coating low houses or houses in which the walls are protected from the winds by a large overhang is not obligatory. In such cases, paint can be applied directly onto the building. Coating the walls does, however, offer certain advantages: it improves the external character of the building by correcting potential problems and by making the color and the texture of the ensemble more uniform; furthermore, smoothing out the walls protects against rain by facilitating the runoff, which allows the dwelling to last longer. Coatings need to be touched up regularly. In South Africa, among the Sotho and Ndebele, for example, it is the women who plaster the house with a mix of clay and cow dung; they know where to find the various soil colors and how to adeptly play with the contrasts. In addition to simple soil coatings, there are coatings of earth mixed with cement, lime, sand, or plaster. The coating creates different textures depending on whether it is smoothed over, scraped, brushed, rubbed, cut, shaped with a trowel, etc.

COLOR AND TEXTURE

Different material treatments—earthen or otherwise—make visible what we call "the material contrast." In fact, the material's color is dependent on the nature and texture of its composing elements.

This specific dimension of apprehending color is closely related to the senses and more specifically to touch. The need to better grasp a color's quality motivates the observer to touch it in order to better perceive soft or rough, smooth or grainy materials.

Color and matter are interdependent and make up a sensorial entity. A single pigmentary composition gives off different color effects on structures whose surfaces are textured differently. Light plays a role in this aspect of the material: in normal lighting conditions, a smooth surface is a lot more reflective than a more light-absorbing rough surface; as a result, the same tone generally appears lighter on a smooth surface than on a structured surface. However, a structured surface seems lighter if read at a light-reflecting angle than if done so at an angle exposed to shade.

Décors and Surfaces

In every country in the world, people lovingly preserve their dwellings. They seek not only to protect materials that risk changing, decaying, or crumbling, they also hope to "make beautiful," to identify with a group or, on the contrary, to mark a distinction, to obey social and religious traditions, or simply to "make clean." We have noticed during our travels that this is one preoccupation that motivates most inhabitants, even those with the most modest homes. In South Africa, for example, we had the opportunity to cross a shanty town in which families from different tribes were housed by neighborhood, and we admired the builders' ingenuity and way of assembling found materials—essentially corrugated sheet metal—and the care taken to decorate their humble shelter with the help of paint, and even interiors with respect to the group's ancestral traditions.

1

1

OPPOSITE 1/2/3

Habitat color is not limited simply to the color of the building material or coating; in certain cases, the color is expressed in designs that convey the residents' desire to beautify their house or affirm their personal or collective identity. Decorative function is a supplement here to the pictorial and chromatic dimension.

These two pages show exterior designs in which the decorative focus displays several levels of "language": in Tarim, South Yemen (1), color accents the moldings on a neoclassical facade; in Zagorsk, Russia (opposite, 3), sculpted wood patterns painted white stand out against the green base of the facade like decorative lace; in Yulian, in the Hangzhou region of China (opposite, 2), two panels painted with landscapes of the nearby Yellow Mountain frame the entryway; in Gournah, near Luxor in Egypt (opposite, 1), residents who have made the pilgrimage to Mecca illustrate the various episodes of their journey in a more narrative fashion.

We will make a distinction between different types of décor. The most simple décor, the most "primitive," consists of working the surface of the soil used to build the walls, or any similar coating, while it is still moist, with the help of a fork, knife, piece of wood, or simply with fingers, which is frequently the case in sub-Saharan Africa. All sorts of patterns, geometric or not, are then drawn on the banco, but the need to re-stucco the surface once a year tends to discourage complex designs. In Niger however, in the Hausa regions, we find a very elaborate type of decorating with patterns in relief drawn from the thickness of the coating. In South Africa and Lesotho, Sotho women trace parallel grooves along the wall to evoke their work in the fields; among the designs they adopt, a predominant floral pattern with four petals, a traditional and symbolic image, is noticeable.

In Lesotho, one can also find décors made with the help of pebbles, which form a sort of basic mosaic, quite austere, that makes reference to the surrounding mountain landscape.

In Burkina, among the Gourounsi, there are still women, assisted by their daughters, who "create colored designs on the exterior walls, composed of red, black, and white geometric designs. For this, they use black pigmenting mud, white kaolin, and red laterites that they hollow out and build up with gourds, pottery shards, and metal strips. Once paint is applied by hand, the shine and brilliance are obtained with a concoction of nerine bulbs."[1]

In regions where builders have different colored stones on hand, exterior design work can be made with the materials themselves. Manipulating them in horizontal bands, vertical chains, friezes, diamonds, checks, etc. presents innumerable variants from one country to the next. In this regard, northern Yemeni architecture is quite remarkable. In Sana'a, the capital city, the color palette for traditional homes comes from the use of different materials: one or two stories of ochre limestone, on which horizontal bands and chains are drawn in black lava, stand on black basalt foundations; pink sandstone and green basalt alternate in arches and lintels. The polychromatic effect of the stone illustrates a very ancient southern Arabic tradition.

1. Manuel Valentin, in *De terre, de paille et de bois: symbolique de l'architecture en Afrique noire.* Paris: Musée de l'Homme, 1998.

Brick is a very practical material for designing an infinite range of décors. Also in Sana'a, brick is used to construct decorative bands on the upper floors. The bricks, shaped into triangles and diamonds, are placed so that they jut out lightly from the wall; in this way, they animate the exterior in a game of structure, game, and composition.

Likewise in Iran, brickwork reaches new heights in ornamental artwork, as their building design attests. As the historian Henri Stierlin recalls: "Everything in Iran starts with simple geometric patterns and develops into a structural game of brickwork, such as it arose toward the end of the ninth century. With the bricks laid horizontally and vertically, jutting out and receding in staggered rows or in fragmented units (half, quarter), it has been possible to attain ornamental solutions of infinite richness and variety, even before getting into polychrome design. The simple rhythm of shadows and the alternating elements allow for the creation of numerous patterns whose variations are related to nomadic rugs . . . Among the designs of this geometric ornamentation based essentially on a principle of repetition, one can cite crosses, diamonds, V-shapes, right-angle patterning, stars, hexagons, octagons, diagonal squares, husks, swastikas, etc." [1]

1. Henri Stierlin, *Isfahan: image du paradis*. Geneva: Sigma, 1976.

1 / 2 / 3

OPPOSITE 1

In South Africa, the Sotho and Ndebele tribes continue to pass on the ancestral tradition of engraving designs on the earthen walls of their homes. From the most simple to the most complex, the decorative pattern may be purely geometrical or, as is the case with the Sotho, a repetitive strip of floral elements.

The use of different colored bricks (whether from their composition or the process of fabrication utilized, or even from a varnish of colored glazing) lends a multiplicity of decorative effects. In Paris, for example, at the Cité Florale (13th arrondissement), brick has led to a whole new combination of moldings and ornamentation which express the builder's attention to architectural detail; striping, friezes, framing, and decorative patterns all take their value from the contrasting tones. On rue des Liserons and rue des Volubilis, certain exteriors are composed entirely of large stripes of different colors.[1]

Mixed masonry, quite popular in Normandy, which works with stone, brick, pebble, and flint, allows for greater freedom of movement for the builder in arranging décors and facades.

As for half-timber construction, many variants are possible depending on country and region, and to often highly desirable decorative effect. In southern Germany, in Franconia, angled overhangs run across each floor and combine ingeniously in criss-crossing patterns. In France, depending on whether you are in Normandy, Alsace, or the Basque region, the pieces of wood exhibit very diverse decorative structures and patterns.

In Pyrghi, a little town on the island of Chios in Greece, there is a unique engraving process used on plaster: the lime-whitened surface is first cut into horizontal strips and then simple patterns based on triangles, circles, half-circles, etc., are created with dry-point engraving.

The white sections inside the pattern are removed with the help of a simple fork to uncover the base layer of black sand mortar. Certain homes are personalized with floral or animal designs drawn all over the door or around the balcony. It is interesting to note that even the undersides of balconies, cornices, and, in general, all structural elements are painted in this way.[2]

1. Jean-Philippe and Dominique Lenclos, "Cité florale: itinéraire chromatique," in *Hameaux: villas et cités de Paris.* Action artistique de la ville de Paris, 1998.
2. Jean-Philippe and Dominique Lenclos, *Couleurs de l'Europe.* Paris: Editions du Monieur, 1995.

1

1

OPPOSITE 1 / 2

In North Yemen, exterior design is a traditional part of architectural language. The geometric patterns painted in limewater combine with a décor formed from a blend of materials in different forms and colors. On the island of Chios, in Greece, Pyrghi testifies to a unique local custom: decorative patterns engraved or cut on white plaster stand out in dark gray on the facade (1 Greece; opposite, 1 / 2 Yemen).

1

1

OPPOSITE 1/2/3
Dwellings with painted designs and patterns are often testimony to the observance of religious traditions; for the Sotho and Ndebele, decorative mural art is a way for residents to summon their ancestors' spirits and ask that they bestow rain and fertility. In Rajasthan, a design of the god Ganesh during a wedding is sure to bring success and fertility upon the newlyweds; in the Thar Desert, near Pakistan, geometric décors are made in honor of Lakshmi, goddess of the home.

(1 Gauteng, South Africa; opposite, 1 Jaisalmer, India; 2 Free State, South Africa; 3 Khuri, India).

Another process in wide use consists of painting directly on the building material or coating. Two South African tribes, the Sotho and Ndebele, craft particularly creative designs on their earthen walls, often emphasizing relief. For the Sotho, traditional colors have a symbolic value: black is associated with ancestors and rain, red and ochres are also used in women's rites of initiation. For the Ndebele, next to earthen-colored designs a very colorful mural may appear with geometric forms highlighted with a thick black line. This relatively recent manner of painting probably corresponds to the desire to differentiate between neighboring tribes. Acrylic paints are used just as often as mineral pigments.

The countries in sub-Saharan Africa where men and women embellish their home exteriors with the help of decorative patterns are quite numerous. We shall mention among them Nigeria, Ghana, Burkina-Faso, Mali, and Mauritania.

In Rajasthan, India, we noted that on several exteriors was a representation of Ganesh, the god with the head of an elephant who brings prosperity to young couples. And in the Thar Desert, near Pakistan, earthen houses are partly covered in large geometric designs made with mineral pigments.

1

Unlike painted and engraved decoration, which requires regular upkeep, patterns made with ceramic tiles seem to be able to defy time with their unalterable matter and color. The term *azulejo* perfectly describes the characteristics of this material: blue in color (*azul* in Portuguese), smooth and shiny (*zulej*). Porcelain tile clay is finer than brick clay and is made of a plastic soil that cooks white, to which kaolin is added to make it even whiter. After a first firing, the tiles are glazed and undergo a second firing. The materials used as colorants are oxides, in particular chromium oxide for green, iron oxide for yellow, orange, and brown, manganese for browns and violets, cobalt for blue, antimony for yellow, copper for green, and tin for white. Portugal is the European country where azulejo is the most often used as exterior surfacing, even on the simplest homes. However, ceramic is one of the principal arts of Arabo-Islamic civiliza-ion, which, in this respect, possesses an important advantage over Western countries.

We shall end this chapter on exterior decoration by noting that the home is often a place of privileged expression for the inhabitants who display their ability, creativity, and talent on walls in a free, spontaneous, and unique fashion. Houses decorated in this way contribute to advancing an inexhaustible and endlessly moving history of folk art, an often modest and unrecognized art form. Certain of these homes have become famous and have been listed on national historical registers, such as the Postman Cheval home in France or the Picassiette home decorated with bits of porcelain by Raymond Isidore. As for the mural decorations of South African artists such as Esther Mahlangu and Francine Ndimande, they are now known worldwide.

2

1

1

OPPOSITE 1 / 2

The Portuguese tradition of azulejo preserves one of the primary arts of Arab-Islamic civlization. This enameled ceramic tile, sometimes in a solid color, but more often decorated, is the basis for an unalterable surface. All types of patterns are possible. Generally, the whole facade is covered in tiles with repetitive patterns that form a decorative ornamentation. Sometimes bands of contrasting colors accentuate the moldings, but there are also ornamental patterns and icons that are inserted into the composition of the house (1 Povoa de Varzim, Portugal; opposite, 1 Povoa de Varzim, Portugal; 2 Paudalho, Brazil).

ANALYSIS OF A SITE

VIVIERS, FRANCE

The site analyses presented in this text are concerned with urban and rural ensembles chosen here and there for their uniformity, or for their significant characteristics in the local use of color as it is applied to the daily habitat. These studies are based on a unique methodology (whose historical aspects were evoked earlier) in order to analyze the different components of the external chromatic palette of dwellings in the most objective way possible.

Beginning with the first studies in 1968, it was obvious how indispensable it was to establish a method that would facilitate apprehending the diverse factors competing in the chromatic makeup of a site. Different sequences of analysis outlined in detail here demonstrate the basic tools for those who are interested in housing colors, beginning with the inhabitants themselves in order to help them understand how color works within a site or a given landscape. This method of analysis was presented in 1982 in our book *Colors of France*,[1] with an inventory of chromatic data collected from about fifteen regions in France starting in 1968. The first results of this investigation were assembled in 1977 under the title "Géographie de la couleur ©," for an exhibit presented by the Center for Industrial Creation at the Georges-Pompidou Center in Paris. Today, this work continues around the world. Within the framework of Atelier 3D Couleur, the work has given rise to multiple applications dealing with color at the regional and rural level at the creation of new towns and industrial complexes, and even in the rehabilitation of older neighborhoods and protected sectors. This has also allowed for the creation of color charts designed for industrial products and synthetic building material such as washes, paints, glass, plastic, and metal.

1. Jean-Philippe and Dominique Lenclos, *Couleurs de la France.* Paris: Editions du Moniteur, 1982.

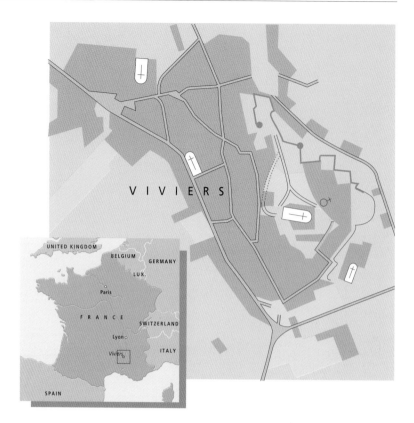

1

1
The city of Viviers, in the Ardèche region, was selected in order to illustrate how a site analysis is carried out. Defensively perched on a hill, the city overlooks the Rhone as it stretches through the vast countryside.

Seen from afar, only the two principal colors of the general palette are apparent: the gray-pink of the canal-tile roofs and the beige of the lime-coated facades.

These photos also illustrate two significant aspects of a site's coloration: the permanent colors of the mineral landscape of the city as a whole and the impermanent colors of the sky, water, and plants of the immediate surroundings.

Certain readers may wonder how we came to choose one site over another. In the course of study and conversation, we acquired a large amount of information about places that seemed to fit our objectives. In certain instances, our choice was made by chance; during our on-site investigations, other sites really stood out.

If, on the one hand, the choice is subjective, the method of site analysis is as objective as possible. As such, when a place has captured our attention, our course of action is generally the following: we select a street or a particularly interesting group of houses in order to make one or more samplings of twenty-five homes. As much as possible, we proceed to our analysis, house by house, in their numbered order, so as to faithfully reproduce what is naturally written into the landscape.

In order to illustrate this method as it unfolds in its successive stages, we have chosen the small town of Viviers, situated in the Ardèche in southeastern France. Why Viviers? It is not a large town—numbering around 3,500 inhabitants—but offers a particularly coherent chromatic and architectural ensemble, as shown in these photos taken from the town's higher elevations.

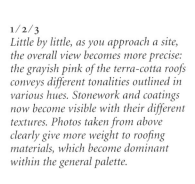

1 / 2 / 3
Little by little, as you approach a site, the overall view becomes more precise: the grayish pink of the terra-cotta roofs conveys different tonalities outlined in various hues. Stonework and coatings now become visible with their different textures. Photos taken from above clearly give more weight to roofing materials, which become dominant within the general palette.

1 / 2 / 3 / 4
These pairs of photos illustrate the important role of the change in seasons; these landscapes were photographed first on January 24, 1997, and then again on June 30, 1998.

Notice the chromatic modifications brought on by the changing light and vegetation.

1

2

3

4

Viviers is an ancient town that has preserved several links to its past. It takes its name from the Latin *vivarium*, for the numerous fishponds (*viviers*) found in the town that nourished reservoirs for the Gallo-Roman town of Alba.

During the Renaissance, the town, prospering from trade, was very much developed and beautified, but the upper town was partly destroyed during the religious wars. The eighteenth century was also prosperous, and the town expanded outside of its medieval ramparts.

The geographic location of this urban center, clustered on a hill overlooking the Rhone and perfectly adapted to its environment, was also an important factor in the choice.

As with many other cities with a historic past, Viviers has for several years been the focus of restoration initiatives in which town planners within the municipal government have mandated the colors of the facades. The town's chromatic physiognomy is currently caught in a transitional phase between spontaneous and imposed colors.

THE SEQUENCE OF STUDY

The analysis takes into account all the elements that contribute to the chromatic character of Viviers' architectural landscape.

It is first of all a question of revealing chromatic specificities and dominant traits of the buildings in their context as seen from a distance.

This is where the notion of *global perception* comes in. Next, when we get closer to the buildings, we switch to the notion of *elemental perception*.

Seen from a certain distance (global perception), the town of Viviers offers a uniform range of color composed of a few dominant tones. This palette, limited to two or three colors, is nonetheless far from meager.

Several factors play a role in the global perception of colors, contributing to the palette's richness:

• Tonal contrasts from one building to the next (both qualitative and quantitative), as well as substance and color contrasts among the materials.

• Volumes and their proportions; they define the architectural language produced in the relationship between full and bare.

• The molding and architectural rhythms; the dominant lines—made up of curves, right angles, horizontals, verticals, and diagonals—help to determine these rhythms and the play between dark and light that they encompass.

• The value contrast found in the brightness scale of the various tonalities.

As is the case with any pictorial work, the colored elements of each house are more or less emphasized by the chromatic quality of the surroundings in which they are inscribed, the colors interacting through a phenomenon of contrasts (Josef Albers has led numerous research projects on this subject[1]).

When we enter the town, little by little as we approach the construction materials, elemental perception reveals a more and more richly detailed vocabulary of colors. In addition, substances and textures express the whole range of their granularity and surface character. This is what Bernard Lassus calls "tactile perception." Thus, a roof of old pink-ochre tiles, having acquired a patina over time, constitutes a veritable tapestry in which each element has it own value, dark or light, and taken individually, each tile is a chromatic universe unto itself.

The color analysis of a site includes two phases:

• On site: an inventory of all chromatic data;

• In the studio: a visual synthesis of our findings from the site.

1/2/3/4
Coating and paint are freshened periodically, bringing about noticeable changes in an urban space based on the residents' choice of color or according to city specifications. The colors evolve, the rhythms change, to such a degree that it is sometimes difficult to recognize the same area after a few years.

1. Josef Albers, *Interaction of Color.* New Haven: Yale University Press, 1987.

CATALOG OF CHROMATIC DATA

The general palette
The dominant architectural chromatics consisting of the roof, wall, and ground coloring represent the greater part of the visible urban space and are designated by the term *general palette*. Roofing, in particular, has a visual importance that tends to be neglected. Differing greatly from country to country or even from one region to the next due to local tradition as well as geological conditions and climate, roofing helps to identify the particularities of an architectural landscape that characterizes the identity of any one country or place. Form and color in roofing have that much more of an effect on the landscape as a whole when they are observed from above, as is the case in Viviers.

Here, the pinkish-beige canal tiles constitute the dominant material. The facades of houses are largely dominated by masonry, in a range of tonalities comprising mainly tinted grays and sand tones. It seems that the tinted grays belong to the older surfaces while the clearer, warmer sand tones are the fruit of recent renovation.

The ground is rarely what one notices first when approaching an architectural site and, in relation to the buildings themselves and to their environment, this spatial dimension is not always perceived with the attention it deserves. Is it simply because the ground is destined for the trampling of feet? Now, during the analysis of a site, when one studies the photos that have been taken of it, one notices that by perceiving the space transposed two-dimensionally on paper, the horizontal surface of the architectural landscape is revealed just as much as the vertical surface. Thus, the slightly trained eye quickly becomes attentive to the visual and sensory importance of the diverse ground treatments. They play an unmistakable role in the identity and personalization of a space and, through their material and color, contribute to the completion of a panorama.

The treatment of ground coverings serves various functions that are often complementary: the utilitarian function of segmentation and spatial location, the signaletic function, which mainly involves security but may also be informational or directional, and the decorative function, obtained through distribution of the colors and substances dictated by the choice of materials. In Viviers, in the old town, the ground evokes traditional materials such as sandstone slabs or pebbles from the Rhone, used alone or in composition. Modern materials such as asphalt and other mortars are equally present in the lower town.

1

2

1/2
These photos, taken the same day before and during the open market, illustrate the importance of random colors in capturing the urban landscape; mobile elements in the everyday setting offer an important counterpoint to the static character of an architectural space.

1

When it is possible, samples of different materials are removed from the terrain. These samples act as initial witness to the substance and color of the various components of the architecture. When sampling is not possible, each color is measured with the help of a color chart.

2/3

A brightness scale, composed of ten segments ranging from white to black, allows for an in situ determination of the mean value of indexed colors. It is notable that vegetable bases are generally closer to black than to white.

4/5

More synthetic than photography, watercolor and colored pencil drawings are the most efficient methods for capturing the principal characteristics of a single dwelling or an architectural ensemble. Indexed next with the help of color charts, each dwelling becomes the object of a synthesizing portrait that illustrates the chromatic components of both the general and the selective palette in the form of a house type. In addition, portraits are also executed in order to demonstrate schematically the quantitative relationship of the various tonalities of each dwelling. The low range represents the qualitative catalog of colors in the ensemble.

The selective palette

The general palette does not adequately convey the chromatic value of a single house or ensemble of residences. Roof and wall colors certainly communicate the dominant coloration of architecture, but they are perfected and often influenced by elements of detail, such as doors, windows, shutters, plinths, and framework, which punctuate the whole with their tinted markings. These accompanying colors comprise the selective palette. Though small in scale, they combine with the general palette to establish a considerably important quantitative relation to bring a structure to life.

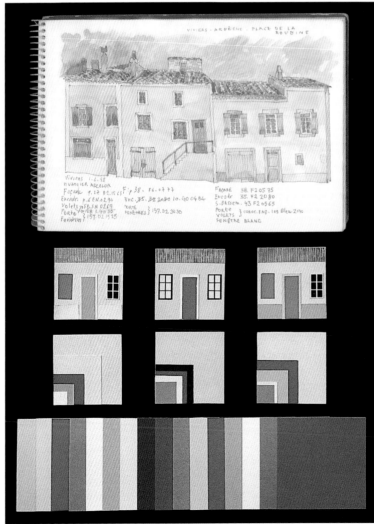

1

IMPERMANENT AND ALEATORY COLORS

The impermanent colors bring into consideration all of the changing elements of a natural landscape: lighting, vegetation, waterways, and sky. Added to these purely geographic factors are other chromatic elements that are subject to change and displacement within the architecture itself or within the immediate surroundings, known as aleatory colors. Changing and unforeseen, they impart a colored movement that animates the architectural landscape: a few geraniums on a windowsill, curtains in windows, shop awnings, and pedestrians themselves acting as a prop of bright and lively colors. Impermanent colors and accidental colors are a counterpart of the static character of architecture. Knowing their importance, these elements factor into on-site study.

The transformations that even the habitat's palette goes through are essentially due to the change in seasons, the succession of plant life, and the fading and renovation of surfaces and materials, added to which is the constant change of light.

Lighting
Light is the basis for seeing color; the visual character of a habitat transforms under the effect of natural light variations throughout the day: it is bluer at noon, redder in the morning or evening. Light varies with seasons as well, its intensity weakens and its color turns more yellow and colder in winter than in summer. Climate and latitude have a determining influence as well on the density and quality of light and, as a result, on how the colors of a given place are perceived. Shadow and

light play off the volume of the architecture, as well as the relief and texture of the materials—roof tiles, stonework, structural surfaces—revealing a building's easily overlooked yet unexpected qualities, even sometimes giving it a magic quality. These games of light determine the contrast values in rhythm with the movement of the sun and clouds across the sky. Shadows accentuate the moldings around architecture, particularly those around doors and windows that structure the exterior.

Aging materials and their renovations
Due to sunlight and weather, materials acquire a patina and progressively age. Terra-cotta tiles discolor and often assume a tone and value comparable to plaster walls, as is the case in Viviers. Periodically renovating the materials causes changes in color that progressively modify the physical layout of the original palette, whether by patching a roof or repairing the facade, a practice performed in regular intervals in certain places. The possibilities for change allowed by painting often give way to very unexpected innovations that bear witness to the inhabitants' desire for individuality that is tied to a real, creative meaning.

Plant elements
The chromatic palette of architecture is very much tied to the plant life that surrounds it. Through their colors and volume, plants are a very important complement to spatial organization. Vegetation stands out against the edifices by the structural and moving character of its foliage, and by the sinuous lines it draws.

Botanic essences, very diverse, offer quite an extensive range of tones in spring and autumn, while in summer this palette reduces itself to a more limited range of greens, which are relatively dark in the shadows cast by shifting foliage. Plant life can, in certain cases, make up a veritable exterior surface and because of this, considerably influence the chromatic palette of the walls.

Parasitic plants that climb up roofs and walls also modify, imperceptibly, the chromatic palette of a dwelling. Moss and lichens add the tint of their brown and green tones, particularly to porous tiles, certain cracking stone, and fibrocement.

As a visual consequence of the use of different materials with specific chromatic characteristics, color in a habitat never stops evolving under the influence of the multiple factors we have just enumerated: aging and renovation of materials, interplay between plant life and the rhythmic tonalities performed by the seasons, continual variations in light both at the quantitative and qualitative level, and the selective contributions of random elements.

1

OPPOSITE 1
Next to the cathedral, the Place de la Plaine, in its sobriety of colors, demonstrates several aspect of palette composition in an urban environment. Here, especially, it demonstrates the strict complement between vegetation color and mineral color, permanence and impermanence. The ground surface displays its own importance in the chromatic ensemble of the landscape. Matter and texture are emphasized the closer the reading is made.

2

1/2
The facades illuminated by the evening light help to highlight the impermanence of color; color touch-ups on the facade, as part of a renovation, expose the contrast in tonalities between older and newer surfaces. The selective palette underscores the architectural language of these urban dwellings.

1/2/3/4
From the pedestrian's perspective, a first glance reveals the house's detailed color vocabulary. Exteriors, whether in exposed masonry or covered by a coating, express their own subtle color and material characteristics. Framing

and carpentry lend to the ensemble more delicate and refined tones.

1

2

3

4

METHODOLOGY

First phase: site analysis

Research progression tends to avoid, as much as possible, a subjective understanding of elements.

Sampling material
In order to work based on the objective data provided by architecture and its environment, we proceed with a meticulous examination of the site by studying the various materials sampled from it, which figure into the composition of ground, walls, roofs, doors, and shutters, and to which foliage, moss, and lichen samplings—the impermanent elements—are added. We note the random attributes that affect the chromatic physiognomy of

a building. Of principal importance to this method, samples constitute an initial observation of colors and material substances. These fragments may seem insignificant in their original context, but they are of great interest when regrouping the documents and reconstituting the chromatic information, an assemblage that will be the basis for synthesizing end results.

Color reproduction
When it is impossible to carry out sampling, color is cataloged either with the help of color guides, or by reproducing the tone with a painted counter-type. We use several color systems simultaneously, some normalized—NCS, Pantone Professional Color Selector, or RAL Design System—others prepared by paint and coating manufacturers. In

addition to this, we have also established our own system of references in our workshop based on the results of our research. This way, we have several thousand colors at our disposal. But we need to be certain to note that in certain cases, this vast enumeration is not always sufficient. We then have recourse to a countertype done in gouache. Color samples can be made with the help of a spectrocolorimeter, and the data are placed in electronic databases. Just the same, we must question the permanence of the data's electronic restitution since it is subject to a quickly and continually evolving technology.

1

1 / 2

In ancient cities, the diversity of materials that have taken on a patina over time or have been freshly renovated articulates the passing of time and participates in the location's poetry.

2

3

4

Sampling the brightness scale of materials
Composed of a regular gradation of ten neutral grays situated between white and black, a linear or circular brightness scale allows us to optically measure the median range of tones in analyzed materials and surfaces. In several cases, the materials do not have a uniform brightness; certain parts are light, others are dark, and it is difficult to determine a median value.

Making a color drawing of the site
A drawing is an efficient way of rapidly capturing a subject and creating a visual synthesis. Color pencils seem to be the most practical tool, since they clearly delineate the tints that make up a chromatic ensemble. Watercolors are likewise recommended for making colored notations of the pattern. Regardless of the technique used, drawings are made on site and not from photos.

Snapshots
Photography cannot always be utilized for a faithful reproduction of colors during the color synthesis of findings, but they are indispensable iconographic documents for remembering, visualizing, and disseminating information.

3 / 4
The ground's visual and tactile importance is too often ignored. The nature of the components, their colors, forms, and proportions create diverse vocabularies depending upon their placement on the ground.

1

In the studio, the colors that were catalogued on site are matched with the corresponding gouache in order to produce synthetic charts. Material sampling is carefully preserved as a testimonial object.

1

A

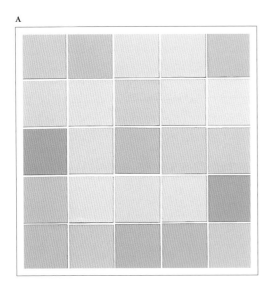

B

C

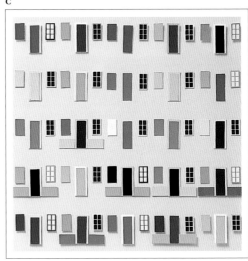

Second phase: the visual synthesis of chromatic findings

The chromatic information obtained from a site is then assembled for the synthesizing phase. Executing this work in the studio requires time and precision. It is necessary to begin with an initial analysis of samples, then transpose this into color charts that reproduce as faithfully as possible the preliminary tonalities.

When it is a question of material samples, one must move away from their chromatic and structural characteristics. Material is, in fact, rarely monochromatic. A brick or coating that has acquired a patina over time brings together an infinite number of nuances that seem difficult to convey in a single color. We can reconstitute the chromatic feel of the material by making a composition of colored marks, but if a simplified reading of the synthesizing chart is desired, only the material's dominating tones as seen from a distance are reproduced. In the first situation, we recreate the color complexity by simply transposing it; in the second, a synthesis is made through a monochromatic flattening out of the colors.

Classifying samples
The samples attained are then classified into several groups:

First group
General palette and selective palette of constitutive elements of each edifice.

A The general palette of exteriors seen from outside the town or village: this reproduces the most important colors of the edifice—facades and roofs.

B The general palette of facades from within the village.

C The selective palette: this takes into consideration the selective elements such as doors, windows, shutters, framework, plinths, etc.

These tables show the results obtained from site analysis in Viviers in June 1998; the first triptych regroups the colors of twenty-five facades as seen from outside the city; the second triptych assembles twenty-five facades notated within the city center, in Place de la Roubine and in adjacent streets.

1
The first chart presents the palette of facade colors in table format.

2
The second chart regroups the various elements from the selective palette: doors, windows, shutters, frames, and foundations.

3
The third chart shows the final result of the site analysis. Here, the elements from the selective palette are superimposed onto the general palette. This synthesizing chart is a historical and geographical notation of an architectural site's chromatic state in a given era.

1

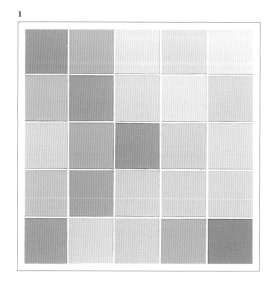

2

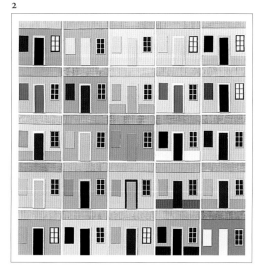

3

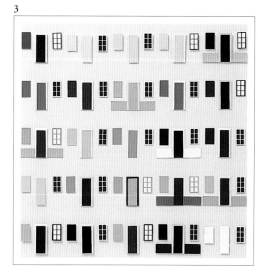

Second group
The palette of qualitative and quantitative relationships.

Samples of similar dimension that make up the catalog of colors for each of the structural elements of a building (roof, walls, doors, shutters, windows) are reassembled into a distinctive palette; this process highlights the qualitative relationship between different tonalities. In addition to this, particularly for representative edifices, the quantitative relationship between tonalities is outlined with charts that are sized proportionally to each of the architectural elements.

Third group
The chromatic palettes comprising the ensemble of an analyzed building, by element:

• roofs
• facades
• framework
• plinths
• doors
• windows
• shutters

The palettes made from these groupings illustrate the dominant colors of each of these elements and allows for the establishment of a visual statistic of the most utilized colors in the site.

1

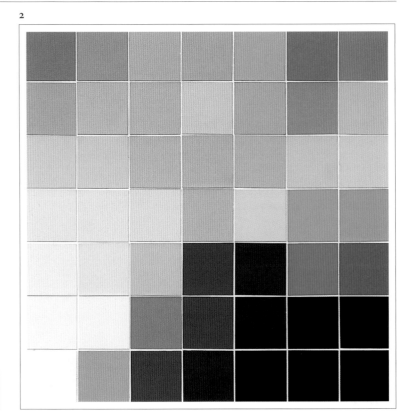

2

3

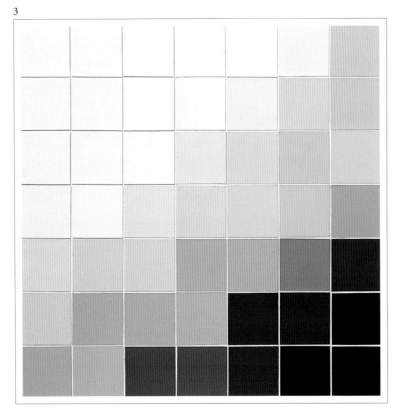

4

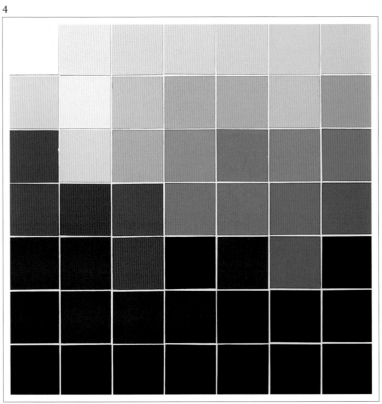

1
The color chart of forty-nine facades arranged on a scale of brightness.

2
The color chart of shutters arranged by lightness and tonality.

3
The color chart of windows.

4
The color chart of doors.

These synthesis charts show the advantage of assembling the qualitative (tonality, clarity, and saturation) and quantitative inventory of a site's architectural color analysis in a practical manner.

1
During site analysis, terrain samples of various materials are taken that figure into the composition of floors, walls, roofs, doors, and shutters. These samples act as an elemental testimony to the color and substance of the architecture's different components; in the studio, they are reproduced with gouache in color samples. Sometimes their tones perfectly match the painting references on established industry color guides.

Synthesis chart
By superimposing the elements of the selective palette onto the general palette, a synthetic reconstitution is obtained for each of the analyzed exteriors. In this way, the twenty-five dwellings catalogued on site are reassembled in the form of a synoptic chart, an objective witness to the site's colors.

The synthesis chart can take several forms:

• *the basic synthesis chart* is composed of twenty-five squares, each one including a door and two windows to which are added roofs, plinths, and shutters. Depending on the circumstances, the exterior elements are represented in a more significant manner for the local architecture: half-timbering, whole centering doors, bands, cornices, etc.

• *the narrative synthesis chart* constitutes another simplified way of representing the colors of the twenty-five exteriors studied, and is used when it proves difficult to take the architectural complexity of the site into account.

In comparing the various synthesis charts, the chromatic specificities of each architectural ensemble studied, from one town to the next, emerge more clearly. The reality of the "geography of color" becomes evident.

In addition, we can imagine that from our results, most of which are dated, comparative studies will be led to highlight the evolution of materials and colors in a given site.

 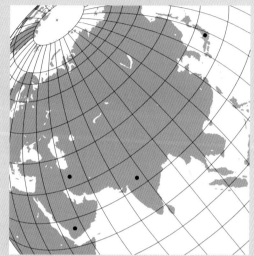 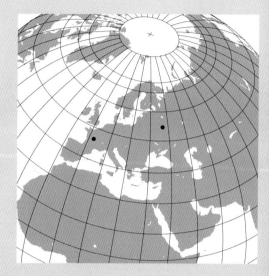

THE UNITED STATES

SAN FRANCISCO

1

In 1848, San Francisco, a small fishing town on a jutting peninsula overlooking the bay, was transformed overnight with the discovery of the first gold nugget. The port had to develop when it rapidly became the most important on the whole West Coast, requiring the creation of a rail system connecting the town to the East Coast and laying the city out on a grid running from the hilltops down to the sea.

On April 18, 1906, a violent earthquake occurred, shaking the whole town and causing terrible fires. Fire destroyed most large buildings and a majority of the 48,000 wooden Victorian houses built to shelter the rapidly growing population. The city was reconstructed immediately and, in 1915, welcomed the international Panama Pacific exposition.

Today, the low, Victorian–style homes rub shoulders with skyscrapers in a cosmopolitan city that brings together Old World charm with New World modernity. These wooden houses are generally qualified as Victorian even though they were constructed in different eras, between 1850 and World War I; they are the pride of their residents who restore them with love, or even reconstruct them entirely. San Francisco can take pride in being the largest city in the world whose habitation is principally Victorian. This type of architecture is the fruit of a rising middle class that benefited from a flourishing economy and from advances in industrial technology.

1
One of the characteristics of San Francisco's chromatic and architectural landscape is the exceptional groupings of numerous Victorian homes built along the hills. Today, there are still between 15,000 and 45,000 that were built between 1850 and 1915. Owners selected their redwood homes, which were built one after another by specialty businesses, from catalogs, giving the owner the ability to tailor the architectural details and color palette to their own tastes (photo taken in 1973).

1

1

*Protecting wood houses requires period-
ically repainting the exterior with
extremely varied colors, allowing for a
change according to owner tastes or
period styles. Black is present in this
palette in San Francisco, as in numerous
Anglo-Saxon cities around the world.*

1

1

1

OPPOSITE 1

Following a series of fires that engulfed entire wood-built neighborhoods in San Francisco, new ordinances required the use of brick in the city center. Iron fire escapes were another answer to residents' preoccupation with safety. This metallic carpentry, light and airy, is usually painted the same color as the facade. The shadows it creates give a unique "language" to the building's moldings.

1

Redwood, available in large quantity, supplies the ideal building material. Supple and easy to cut, it allows for the most varied forms and imaginative ornamentation, chosen from catalogs by the owners and used to decorate facades in the most personal and creative ways. With their turrets, colonnade entryways, stained glass, and geometric and floral designs, the Victorian houses of San Francisco have a very specific architectural character and no two homes are ever alike. The most frequent style is Stick-Eastlake, which owes its name to the English architect Locke Eastlake and to the cornices ("stick"), crown doors, and windows,

the Italianate style inspired by the Italian Renaissance with its squared windows and narrow doorways, and the Queen Anne style, identifiable by pointed roofs, porches, and turrets, the dominant style in England around 1860. The Queen Anne–style homes situated in Alamo Square and built by Matthew Kavanough between 1884 and 1895 are the most famous in San Francisco. All the residences share a common trait, regardless of their style: the bay window, a protruding window which has the advantage in this frequently foggy city of brightening and cleaning rooms, while at the same time enlarging them.

Victorian homes are commonly known as "Painted Ladies." Since the wood requires solid protection in order to withstand the aggressive sun, fog, and humidity, as early as 1850 painters used paints with different tonalities in order to make the various parts of the home stand out: the ground floor was one color, the second floor another, and so forth. The intended objective was above all to underscore the architecture: "Painting is a matter of protection, chiefly, but is of most vital importance also in regard to the beauty of a house."[1]

1. E. C. Hussey, 1874, in M. Larsen and E. Pomada, *Painted Ladies: Those Resplendent Victorians.* New York: E. P. Dutton, 1978.

1

1 / 2

OPPOSITE 1

As the city's architectural legacy, the Painted Ladies are protected today by local associations that favor regular renovation and repainting. Walking down the slopes of Pierce Street and Pacific Avenue, there are always worksites to be found, often with surprises in store in terms of tonalities. The random car colors are sometimes in perfect chromatic harmony with the permanent colors of the neighborhood. Perhaps this isn't simply coincidental.

2

1

1/2
OPPOSITE 1
Small towers, cornices, railings, and columns—so many ornamental elements characterize each of these facades. These decorative pieces were mass-produced after the arrival of steam-driven woodcutting machines. The houses, as different as they are, all have bay windows, which expand the rooms and allow for more light.

2

1

However, during the first half of the twentieth century, the facades of Victorian homes were neglected and fell into disrepair; during World War II, they were even whitewashed with the surplus of dull gray paint intended for battleships! It was necessary to wait until the 1960s and the advent of the San Francisco Colorist movement to see the rebirth of the Painted Ladies in all their chromatic splendor—red, yellow, blue, chocolate, walnut, pink—every eccentricity was permitted. The reasons for this movement were multiple: we can see a response to the dehumanization brought on by technology and the construction of monolithic towers, inhabitants' need to express their creativity and individuality, and the desire to preserve past heritage by giving it a new vitality. The "face-lift" of San Francisco's Victorian homes began with groups of designers such as Blissful Painting, Flying Colors, and Color Control. In the presence of renovations that blended up to twenty-four different colors on a single exterior, Foster Meagher, artist, designer, and colorist, conceived of relatively moderate chromatic palettes, keeping in mind the building's history, its location, exposure to the sun and bad weather, and the impact of the new scale on the urban environment. His color schemas included five tonalities that correspond to five architectural functions.

In his work *Colour Outside,*[1] Tom Porter defines the functions in this way: First, a background "body" color—usually of high lightness value—which occupies flat wall surfaces. Second, a color he describes as "architectural," i.e., one of high chroma which will delineate any visible working parts such as plinths, corbels, columns, etc. Third, individual or pairs of target colors—usually strong hues—used to pick out door panels, linear framing, moldings, etc. Fourth, a dark color of low value employed when necessary as a "shadow" to help large, unattractive areas recede. Finally, a fifth color is also held in reserve—a color high in lightness value used, when required, to project any additional architectural finery of note.

1. Tom Porter, *Colour Outside*. London: The Architectural Press, 1982.

Numerous associations have been created to encourage the owners of Victorian homes to restore them with respect to their architectural character. For these organizations, it is a question of investing in the future by saving the past. For example, FACE (Federally Assisted Code Enforcement) and RAP (Rehabilitation Assistance Program) have allowed certain residents of Alamo Square to restore their homes to a state of elegance by unblocking public funds.

Our color study, conducted in August of 1987 along Pierce Street and Pacific Avenue, focused on Victorian houses that certain purists would not place among genuine Painted Ladies. However, referring back to Larsen and Pomada, we can determine that the houses studied correspond to defining criteria as follows: ". . . that the Victorian building be a balanced, felicitous blend of color and architecture; that the house be painted in three or more contrasting colors; and that color be used to bring out the decorative ruffles and flourishes."

1 / 2 / 3 / 4
Among the Victorian homes, there are sometimes more modern residences. Their colors are sober and outlined in white.

1

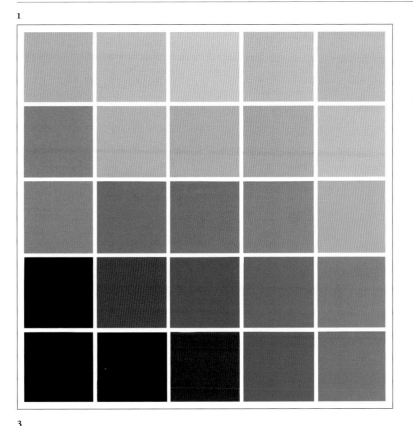

2

3

1 / 2

These two tables summarize the colors that were recorded in San Francisco along Pierce Street and Pacific Avenue in 1987. The table at left, of exterior colors, underscores the dominant sand tones and tinted grays, which are augmented with a few dark tones— brown, black, and dark green. The synthesizing table on the right combines the general palette and selective palette, and demonstrates a half-tint coloration outlined in the white carpentry work.

3 / 4

At the end of the 1860s, the Italianate style started to appear, inspired by the Italian Renaissance. It is identifiable by the architectural detailing around cornices and the frames of rotunda windows and doors. With little contrast on a scale of brightness, these homes nonetheless assert a chromatic identity that is accentuated by alternating warm and cold colors.

4

GREENWICH VILLAGE

Greenwich Village, known in New York as "the Village," is a neighborhood that, along with Wall Street, the Bowery, and Chinatown, makes up southern Manhattan, the oldest part of the city. At the end of the seventeenth century, this area, first colonized by the Dutch who supplanted the Indians, was occupied by the British who gave it the name "Greenwich."

1

1
These exterior surface samples, taken in Greenwich Village in 1983, testify to the color and material used in this New York neighborhood at that time. It is interesting to note how simple bits of color can so significantly illustrate the chromatic atmosphere of a cityscape and reconstitute an essential aspect of the memory of a place.

1 / 2
These two snapshots, taken on Washington Place in 1983 and 1997, respectively, highlight both the impermanence of color as well as the important role that random colors play in an urban site. Vehicles, awnings, and pedestrians act as ephemeral supports to the changing tones.

The Village was a rural farming zone until part of the land owned by wealthy New Yorkers was transformed into lots, because of the expansion of New York. In addition, at the beginning of the nineteenth century, residents from the port, fleeing smallpox and yellow fever epidemics, considered the Village a safe haven, impressively increasing the population. In spite of the urban planning of 1811 that envisioned a grid for Greenwich Village, the new residents built their homes along well-traveled routes, thereby creating the sinuous lines of certain streets.

During the 1820s, two- and three-story brick buildings filled the Village's narrow streets in order to accommodate a population comprising mostly middle-class families, merchants, and specialized workers. At the same time, a massive wave of immigration shaped the neighborhood, causing its surroundings to degrade rapidly; it was then that the Village began to attract young artists for its calm, isolation, and modest rents. With the construction of Seventh Avenue and the arrival of the subway, the isolation became quite relative. Just the same, Greenwich Village remains a neighborhood apart, a unique place, a sort of small preserved island full of charm in the heart of the large city.

1

2

1

1
Within the heart of Greenwich Village, Greene Street offers a series of apartment buildings with cast-iron armature and facades, dating from the 1850s and 1860s. These facades have taken on contrasting colors that assert a rhythm within this urban environment.

1

2

4

3

1 / 2 / 3 / 4
The Village, where artists and writers live, is a privileged neighborhood with its calm little streets lined with buildings that rarely reach beyond three stories. These brick apartment buildings, sometimes painted, have a coloration that recalls the chromatic palette of older English and Dutch cities (1 / 2 Bleecker Street; 3 Bedford Street; 4 Gay Street).

1

1

OPPOSITE 1
The grouping of identical homes, or row houses, displays a certain austerity both on the architectural and chromatic levels. Whether they are left with the natural material, brick, or painted, these residential buildings testify to a certain elegance brought about by the architect's attention to architectural and color detail. The selective palette of the white-trimmed windows and doors emphasizes the color of the material or coating. Coating the facades helps to personalize them.

1

Our color study, conducted in July of 1983, dealt principally with Sullivan, Christopher, and Bedford Streets, each composed of rows of brick houses. On facades painted in contrasting tones, external fire escapes, with their sober colors, form a distinctive repetitive weave. Houses built at the beginning of the nineteenth century incorporate a rather uniform style with their two floors and their steep dormer roofs. On the brick facade, stone rarely intervenes: door and window lintels are done in marble and sandstone.

The entryway in painted wood is the only visible sign of wealth, with its Georgian style and its frame of Doric or Ionic columns supporting the architrave. A third floor often replaced mansards and a new cornice was then added to the front of the building. This, as with other elements of the selective palette, contrasts with the very light, or conversely, very dark tones of the exterior material.

This reveals that the specificity of the materials and their colors is narrowly tied to even the molding of the neighborhood's architecture, which confers a very particular character. Despite a rich and composite palette, Greenwich Village expresses a coherence and uniformity that is quite contingent on the scale of the buildings, thus establishing a very personalized and harmonious urban space. This is a particularly significant example of color attributes in the identity of urban heritage.

1

2

3

1 / 2 / 3
The colors in Soho and Greenwich Village are often dominated by deep red and gray brick tones. These relatively somber tones are often broken up with white, cream, or light gray, giving a strong personality to the New York City landscape (1 Greene Street; 2 / 3 Bleecker Street).

1

2

1 / 2
*Fourteen years separate these photos
of Sullivan Street. Once again, you
can notice the important role of
impermanent colors in the urban
landscape.*

1

1

1

OPPOSITE 1

One of the unique elements of New York architecture from the nineteenth century is the presence of metal stairways that form a netting structure around the exterior. These fire escapes became mandatory, for security reasons, after a huge fire in 1835. The *shadows of this light armor create a graphic and rhythmic language that changes throughout the day (1 Bleecker Street; opposite, 1 Christopher Street).*

1

1
The light in New York, which is on the same latitude as Naples and Istanbul, is so intense that it creates phenomenal plays of shadow and light, cutting up the urban space and accentuating its contrasts. An average street corner thus becomes a pictorial composition juxtaposing graphic signs, materials, and colors.

1

2

3

4

1 / 2 / 3 / 4
The facades of Greenwich Village, with their very graphic architectural language, are reinforced by contrasting light and dark, warm and cold tones. Black and gray are quite present.

1

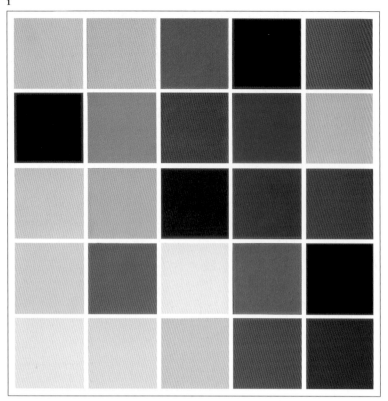

2

3

4

1 / 3

These two charts regroup, on the one hand, facade colors (general palette) from apartment buildings studied in Greenwich Village, and on the other, the overall synthesis of these facades, which combines the general and selective palettes. This analysis, which dates from 1983, reveals the presence of dark and light colors, distributed evenly. The dark tones are a mix of reddish-browns, blacks, and grays, while the light tones range from white to light green, ivory, and sand tones.

2 / 4

These two sketches were made on Washington Place and at the corner of Bleecker Street and Fifth Avenue. Colored-pencil drawings allow us to outline the chromatic components of the architecture in a practical way and to facilitate their synthesis.

1 / 2
Perceiving a site's colors depends on the reading distance. From a pedestrian's perspective, colors help the material texture—in this case brick, whose joints form a regular pattern—stand out.

1

2

OPPOSITE 1
San Francisco and New York are far from limited to a few types of facades. We have focused on a few Painted Ladies from San Francisco, Victorian houses whose owners often renew their chromatic makeup.

In New York, Greenwich Village was chosen for its uniformity of architectural scale and chromatic palette. These illustrations articulate the marked contrasts that create a rhythm in the sequence of facades and colored punctuation of detail elements.

1 / 2 / 3 / 4
Sullivan Street's apartment buildings are witness to the postcolonial era that was inspired by English neoclassicism. Particularly refined entryways are framed with lateral windows; often crowned with a fanned archway, they

are generally dark-colored and framed in immaculate white. The facade surfaces, black, gray, and brick red punctuated by white, evoke the chromatic spectrum of certain London and Amsterdam streets.

GUATEMALA

In 1984, when we visited Guatemala, this beautiful Latin American country was, and already had been for twenty years, the scene of bloody skirmishes between the Indians and the military leaders in power. From Mexico where she was in exile, Rigoberta Menchú, a young Indian, was bravely fighting so that her people could acquire a dignified life and respect for their own identity. In 1992, five hundred years after the arrival of Christopher Columbus, she won the Nobel Peace Prize "for her contribution to social justice and to the reconciliation of different ethnic groups."

1

1
Antigua, the former capital of Guatemala, was destroyed several times by earthquakes, as certain buildings still in ruins attest, hinting to its magnificent past. Setting the baroque monuments aside, we shall focus on the enchanting chromatics emanating from this street lined with modest dwellings against the backdrop of the volcano's verdant slopes.

1 / 2
The frequent use of certain colors in certain cultures is surprising. These photos show a dominance of turquoise-blue and yellow tones on the facades, highlighting the concept of a geography of color.

The bright contrasts, clearly favored by the residents, shows how, in the language of colors, the chromatic palette's tonal composition is representative of a population's cultural tastes and identities (1 Solola; 2 Antigua).

1

2

Situated to the south of Mexico is this relatively small country whose name means "land of trees" in the native language, a country with a wide variety of landscapes, a central section of highlands framed by two mountain chains that form a natural climatic border and stretch out in a series of terraces whose character varies by altitude. Several recent volcanic eruptions (some volcanoes are still active) have widely influenced the country's history, most notably by forcing the displacement of the capital city. In northern Guatemala, the Petén, a low-altitude limestone plateau with a hot, humid climate, is home to a vast tropical forest where magnificent vestiges of Mayan civilization are guarded by brightly colored birds and monkeys who chase each other through the trees.

With such dissimilar natural settings, agriculture varies greatly from place to place. In the highlands, on minuscule plots of land, Indians cultivate the corn, wheat, and vegetables necessary for the country's sustenance. The large, modern plantations in the hotter regions produce sugarcane, cotton, cocoa, and bananas; coffee is cultivated up to an altitude of 5,900 feet (1,800 meters). Each of these crops, and more recently fruits and vegetables, is intended for export. Other economic sectors, such as a quality meat industry, as well as oil and nickel operations, are currently on the rise.

Despite its natural riches, Guatemala has been weakened for decades by one basic problem: land division. In fact, land belongs to a minority of landowners while the Indian population, even though they form a majority in the country, is limited to seasonal work on large plantations or, depending on the settlement, profits from acting as usufructuaries, those who hold small parcels of land in exchange for working several jobs for the proprietor. Indians have no power against the "Ladinos" and are subject to a racism that is deeply rooted in the national mindset. The problem is much more crucial nowadays as the population rapidly expands, especially among the Indians.

The term *Ladino* designated, at the time of Spanish colonization, any Indian who spoke perfect Catalan. For Indians today, Ladino is the white man, and more broadly, any Guatemalan who claims Spanish heritage, rejecting Indian values and not speaking any of the Mayan dialects. These are two opposing cultures, two worlds colliding.

In the religious arena, there is a sort of syncretism, noticeable in Indian communities, between Catholicism inherited from Spanish colonization and the ancient Mayan religion, notably in the rituals that accompany the cultivation of corn. In fact, corn is not only a basis for food, it is also an essential religious symbol.

"The Mayas can truly say that they are what they eat. They believe that the gods have fashioned them out of ground corn and, ever since, that plant is their basic sustenance from dawn to dusk, from birth to death. Living consists of planting corn—making *milpa*—in order to cultivate golden *gracia*, divine grace.

1

2

3

4

The cycle of corn, from which even the name *Maya* is derived, governs their year more firmly than our seasons. The care of corn crops in the field is a sacred duty for men, just as preparing it in the hearth is the sacred duty of women."[1]

In the Popol Vuh, we also discovered that the colors, which still play such an important role today in architecture and artisanry, carried a well-defined symbolic weight in the particular vision of the land and its place in the universe. In fact, the gods of creation attributed a specific color to each of the four corners of the world: red to the East where the Sun god rose, black to the West where each evening the sun disappeared into frightful shadow, yellow to the South for the sun at its zenith, and white to the North from where change and winds blow, bringing rain. And at the center of this diamond is the fifth vital color: the blue-green of water and fertility. In Tikal, for example, the temples are painted red, the color of the sun and of blood, the drink of the gods.

1. Jeffrey Becom and Sally Jean Aberg, *Maya Color: The Painted Villages of Mesoamerica.* New York: Abbeville Press, 1997.

1 / 2 / 3 / 4

OPPOSITE 1 / 2 / 3 / 4

On these two pages, you can see the range of external colors and notice how the predominant solid tonalities alternate with warmer and cooler shades (Solola, Antigua, Jocotenango).

Along the road, in markets and during religious festival, colors explode in traditional Indian outfits in the brightest, most luminous tones. Traditional dress remains one of the most expressive manifestations of cultural affirmation for the Mayas; it is a veritable identity card since styles, patterns, and colors vary with the age, social status, and place of origin of whomever is wearing the garment. The weave blends ancient themes with new ones and Mayan patterns and symbols with colonial ones. Despite the arrival of machine-made fabrics, most clothing is hand-woven. All Indian women have their weaving tasks and they dedicate all of their talent and care for months to making magnificent *huipils* by hand, weaving and embroidering geometric patterns and stylized birds or flowers in bursting color, reflecting their love of nature.

Modern dyeing has progressively replaced the traditional vegetable-, animal-, and mineral-based dyes used since the pre-Columbian era. The color violet, extracted from a mollusk, the *Purpura patula* found along the coasts of Costa Rica and Nicaragua, gives fabric a very special value. This is the color of religious holidays.

If the smallest details of the chromatic richness of Indian clothing caught our attention, down to the brightly colored ribbon woven through braids of long, black hair, we did not go so far as to forget the color of habitations, which was the primary objective of our trip. It is necessary to distinguish the architecture in towns and villages from the architecture found in the countryside. Rural architecture is poor, generally limited to thatched cottages with a straw or palm-leaf roof that includes a single bedroom for the whole family and a small kitchen where a fire is made on the floor on a bed of stones. In the mountains, at high altitudes, the hovels are even more meager and more precarious, the walls being made from a mixture of earth, fiber, roots, and whatever else falls in the hands of the builder.

1

2

3

1

1

OPPOSITE 1 / 2 / 3

While crossing the small town of Salcaja on August 16, 1984, on our way to Atitlan Lake, we were surprised by the dominant turquoise tones that covered most of the residences. Once again, we were witnessing the manifestation of a geography of color! Will we ever know why turquoise blue is so sought after? We must nevertheless recall that for the Mayas, blue-green was one of the five vital colors, both the color of water and fertility.

1

1
The bright contrast of these two shop fronts in Solola is the backdrop for the market. Here, the permanent colors of the ground and architecture mix with the random colors of the local costume, which are an exceptional articulation of indigenous culture in this country.

2
The huipil, a blouse worn by native women, is woven with care and embroidered with geometric designs, as well as stylized birds and flowers. The blend of colors and patterns reveals ethnic group, age, and social standing. This antique huipil embroidered with geometric designs comes for the province of Quiché.

2

An evolution is, however, coming to light, favoring adobe homes, or sun-dried brick, coated in mud plaster before being painted. Towns and villages in the highland regions are very ancient settlements; most of them were already populated by the Mayas before the arrival of the Spanish and have remained quite faithful to their traditions and local dialect. In small localities, the low houses here and there along the road are simple parallelepipeds in adobe or in cement washed in bright colors, dominated by a light emerald green, blue, and yellow ochre. In Mayan hamlets and villages, residents who feared causing envy among their neighbors and being treated like Ladinos often used color paints quite sparingly. In fact, whether of mixed or pure, indigenous blood, they have left behind their Indian dialects, customs, and dress in order to adopt a Spanish mentality, even down to how they paint their homes. Ladinos cover their street-side facades with brazen colors to call their neighbors' attention to their wealth.

Color, in this way, becomes the symbol of a certain power, a lower-class power, however, that is scorned by the country's elite whose lavish homes are painted in white. We completed two color samplings, in the village of Salcaja, near Quezaltenango, and in the small town of Solola, which is crossed in order to reach Chichicas-tenango and which overlooks one of the world's most beautiful lakes, Lake Atitlan. On market days, Indians from neighboring villages come together in their traditional dress: a red, flowered huipil for women and, for men, striped pants worn with a short vest. The cemetery is remarkable, with tombs pained in the same bright colors used for the homes of the living, most definitely with the same paint can.

Also on Lake Atitlan, across from the San Pedro volcano, the small town of Santiago Atitlan remains faithful to its vestmental traditions with, for women, a red skirt with white and navy designs, a huipil embroidered with colored animals and flowers, and a headdress made of several feet of wound red ribbon, and, for men, pants with white and purple bands embroidered with bird designs.

1 / 2 / 3
The frequent presence of yellow on the walls of Mayan dwellings is undoubtedly a reflection of the color of corn, the vital and sacred plant from which "Maya" is derived. It is also the color of the south and of the sun at its zenith.

1

1

OPPOSITE 1/2
In Mayan villages, the cemetery is traditionally a place where residents give free rein to their creativity by using exuberant colors.

Solola cemetery is oriented to the south, contrary to the tradition of orienting the tombstones to the east, facing the rising sun. One of the dominant colors is blue-green, a symbol of water, of growing corn, and thus, of fertility and life.

All the other colors of the habitat can also be found in the cemetery, but on the tombstones these colors thrive with even greater extravagance and freedom than on the houses (Solola).

Surrounded by three volcanoes that periodically threaten it, Antigua, the former capital of Guatemala, was founded in 1543 following the destruction of Santiago de los Caballeros by a terrible flood. In 1773, Antigua, built on the country's main seismic fault and already victim to numerous earthquakes, was seriously damaged by a new quake and abandoned in favor of the current capital, Guatemala City. Partially restored, Antigua hints at its two centuries of being one of the most beautiful cities in Spanish America. Its architecture has been adapted to the risk of earthquakes; its buildings with their low profile of thick rubble walls, low arches, and wide pillars would seem heavy if it were not for light-colored surfaces and a proliferation of Baroque–style decorative elements that imbue them with charm. Streets drawn at right angles and radiating from the central square are bordered by pink stucco homes decorated with bougainvillea. This magnificent town has been registered as a cultural site on the worldwide heritage index since 1979.

Quezaltenango, the capital of Altos, is the most important city after Guatemala City. It has preserved its colonial heritage with narrow streets and homes with windows protected by grills; the entire surrounding region, the first to have been occupied by the Spanish, possesses the oldest buildings of the colonial era. Lastly, there is Chichicastenango, where the Popol Vuh, the Mayan Quiché bible, was found. Saint Thomas Church, built by Dominicans in the sixteenth century and a place of worship as pagan as it is religious, dominates the market square where the Indians from neighboring villages meet in flaming fabric colors in stalls in order to sell the fruit of their agricultural and artisanal labor. With its paved streets, colored houses, and red-tiled roofs, it is a small town with much charm.

A country of intense colors both in nature and in architecture, not to mention its textile artisanry, a country of contrasts in which the grandiose beauty of the countryside coexists with a wild release of elements, and the silent reserve of the Indian people coexists with ardent revolt against oppression and injustice, Guatemala is endearing and fascinating.

2

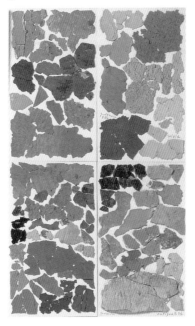

4

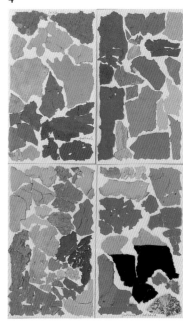

1

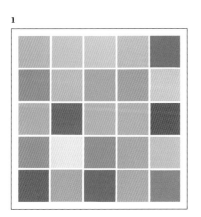

3

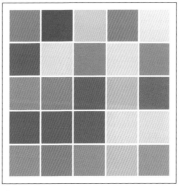

5

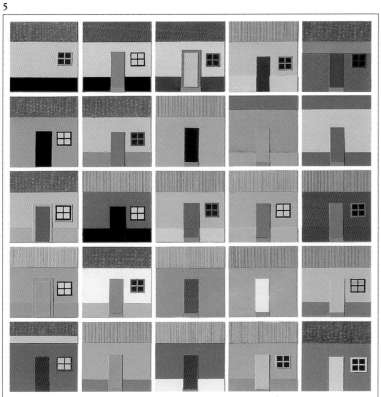

6

These watercolors show a few archetypes of Guatemaltec homes from the high plateaus. The top two rows illustrate the style of dwellings in Antigua, the former capital of Guatemala, where foundation colors most often contrast with the facade;

woodwork around windows and doors is also painted in contrasting tones. The three houses in the bottom row are village houses where solid blues and turquoise dominate, as is the case in Salcaja.

1 / 2 / 3 / 4 / 5 / 6
This page brings together results from studies in two small Guatemaltec cities: to the left, Solola, in Quiché province, and to the right, Salcaja, in Quetzaltenango province. Comparing these two palettes, we can see marked differences (in Solola, the facades show

more varied and contrasting colorations than in Salcaja) as well as similarities, essentially in the prevalence of blue, green, and turquoise-blue.

BRAZIL

SALVADOR DE BAHIA

The city of Salvador, capital of the state of Bahia, is situated at the entrance to the Bahia de Todos os Santos, the Bay of All Saints (so called because it was discovered around All Saints Day, November 1, 1501).

Founded in 1549 by the Portuguese, Salvador was for centuries the civil, religious, and military capital of Brazil; it offered the advantage of its exceptional geographic location, raised up on a peninsula, therefore easily defendable, in the heart of an immense, sheltered bay. All around the city, massape, made of black clay, was an excellent soil for cultivating sugarcane, which, along with tobacco, brought wealth to the city until the great crisis of the 1680s. Despite a certain decline, a life of feasts and luxury continued until the end of the eighteenth century, not without recalling the ambiance that reigned during the same period in the cities of Minas Gerais.

Today, the city, which comprises more than two million inhabitants, is essentially made up of blacks, descendants of slaves brought from Africa in the sixteenth and seventeenth centuries to work the plantations. Certain neighborhoods are poor and, when the paint chips on homes painted in bright colors or pastels, the damp and leprous walls can be glimpsed. But, under the Bahia sun, color, music, and the joie-de-vivre of the Bahian people lend the streets an air of permanent celebration. A fair number of Bahian people continue to wear the famous local dress: the *Baiana-nago* is adorned in a brightly colored, floral skirt and a relatively low-cut blouse with short, wide sleeves, while the *Baiana-muçulmana*, originally from Sudan, is dressed in a large, flowing white robe.

Religious and popular festivals hold great importance in the lives of Bahian people and nourish their mysticism and liveliness. Compared to Catholic ritual, the *candomble* celebration has made considerable gains over the last thirty years. It is a time for invoking the *orixas*, incarnations of good and bad forces of nature that hid for a long time behind the images of saints. Different colors characterize each of them: white for Oxala, green for Oxassi, yellow for Oxum, red and white for Xango, white and light blue for Yemanja, etc.

1

1
Pelourinho Square is the historic heart of Salvador's old districts. Registered on the list of humanity's cultural heritage, it is the focus of attentive care in building restoration and maintenance. Because of the effects of the high humidity, the pastel tones on the facades are repainted regularly following a coloration scheme designed by architects in the Artistic and Cultural Heritage Foundation of Bahia.

The city of Salvador stretches over 5 miles (12 kilometers) on a steep hill. A cliff, reaching up to 230 feet (70 meters) in height in some spots, separates the lower town from the upper town. In the beginning of colonization, the authorities—governor generals, bishops, the first Jesuits, top-ranking officials—moved into the upper town, whose jagged terrain offered a natural protection against attacks by Indians. The object of urban planning, Salvador presents a unique ensemble of rectilinear paths and rectangular public squares.

While the lower town is home to commerce and harbor operations, the upper town has remained the administrative, religious, and cultural center. The *cidade alta* houses the old city with its beautiful Baroque buildings where, in the eighteenth century, the merchants who thrived on the export of sugar and tobacco, and on the slave trade, lived.

In Bahia, in the old quarter, the churches are innumerable. Legend has it that there were as many as there were days in a year; in reality, there are only one hundred and fifty. The cathedral, a former church of the Jesuit school, is coated in lioz, a very beautiful material imported from Portugal, which also served in the construction of the Church of Pilar in a very simple style with elegant proportions. If most churches exhibit a relatively sober exterior character, this is not the case for the Ordem Terceira de São Francisco Church, decorated with *almofada* pilasters, or relief ceilings, and with typical decorative patterns also found on the entirely sculpted facade of the Ordem Terceira do Carmo Chapel.

1 / 2 / 3
Two steps away from the Salvador cathedral, these old facades are the site of the contrasting colors of the restoration project. Frames, moldings, and cornices, uniformly white, outline the structural unity of the ensemble (Cruzeiro de São Francisco).

1 / 2 / 3

Freshly repainted in delicate colors, these homes in Pernambuco testify to the care that residents give to exterior upkeep. With sculpted cornices, the buildings reflect architectural traditions in Portugal.

4 / 5

These photos, taken in 1979 and 1998, respectively, eloquently demonstrate the spectacular transformation a house undergoes when it is left in disrepair. Different layers of colored coatings are visible.

In terms of color, the blue church of Nossa Senhora do Rosario dos Pretos, the slave church, would be more surprising if it were not in the heart of the restored old city, in Pelourinho plaza. This triangular piazza, a theater for the torture inflicted upon slaves up until the suppression of the pillory in 1835, has regained its original character comprising twenty-seven homes of notable citizens, with exteriors painted in pure colors—greens, ochres, blues, and pinks—with respect to tradition and under the direction of Bahia's Artistic and Cultural Heritage Foundation.

The neighborhood of Pelourinho, where we conducted our first study, in 1979, has been protected by the Patrimonio Historico Nacional since the 1940s. Since 1993, a large number of homes have been carefully restored and repainted in harmonious pastel tones of light and dark blue, yellow, pink, green, and ochre. The canal-tile roofs add their warm, brownish-orange tones to an already rich general palette. The houses, which are pretty tall, are remarkable for their simplicity and the uniformity of their architectural patterning. Openings, while few in number, are decorated with framework that is often embellished with decorative molding and relief work.

In February 1998, during a second trip, we noticed the important transformation the neighborhood had undergone, becoming a place of intense tourist activity. Happily, a few streets nearby have maintained their dwellings and authentic character. The selective palette is more somber than the general palette, especially in the restored section of the old city, where it is limited to a few colors: centering window and door frames are generally white, sometimes beige ochre, as are the corner edges and horizontal strips that outline the frames of the facade. Windows are white; as for doors, they are mainly dark to medium green.

It is a shame that, in this restoration, the selective palette has been reduced to these few colors; in fact, the neighborhoods that have not yet been renovated display a wider variety in the choice of tonalities: there are doors in medium blues and ochres, as well as very soft grays, whites, and greens that are unique to the chromatic character of the town.

1 / 2
In these villages of the Nordeste, Cachoeira and Vittoria, row houses create a rhythm within the urban environment with their lively and contrasting colors. In Cachoeira (Bahia State) each facade asserts its own identity in personalized designs and palettes.

1

2

3

4

1 / 2 / 3 / 4
*These four photos, taken in 1998, show
different aspects of urban coloration in
Pelourinho and its outlying areas,
sometimes discreet in subtle cameo,
sometimes assertive in rich, saturated
colors. Notice the consistent use of
white in the selective palette.*

1

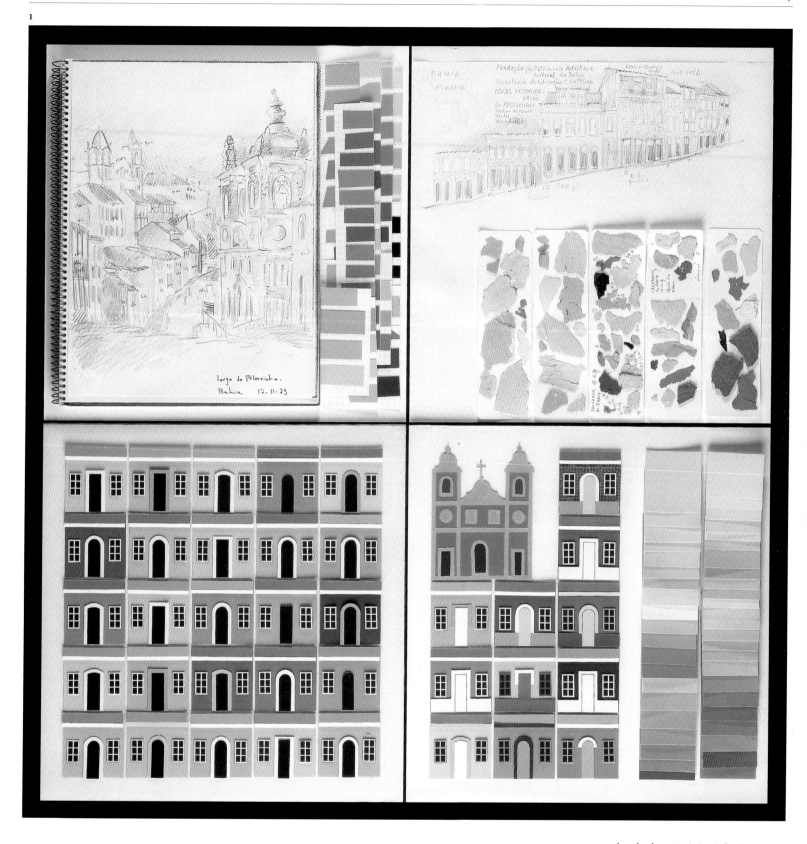

1

This chart is a summary of a study carried out in 1979 in the Pelourinho quarter in Salvador (Bahia State). This synthesis, regrouping thirty-six colors recorded in Pelourinho and the adjacent streets, is a historic testament of the dominant pastel tones that were already characteristic at the time (sketch by Jean-Jacques Terrin).

PERNAMBUCO

RECIFE AND OLINDA

When we arrived in Olinda on February 14, 1998, we arrived to full-out Carnival preparations. All night long nothing could be heard but music and laughter and nothing could be seen but people climbing platforms in haste to join the festivities.

1

1

The canal-tile roofs of Olinda are seen here from above, which is possible because this old colonial city is perched on hills overlooking the Atlantic Ocean. You can make out the cool and contrasting tones that are *characteristic of the palette for this extraordinary site, which is registered with UNESCO.*

In Olinda, Carnival lasts for eleven days, beginning during the week before the official opening, which is marked by parades with students from the large dance schools. It is a popular carnival with a reputation known throughout Pernambuco and even all of Brazil. Thousands of people in costume, children and adults, white and black, rich and poor, passionately dance the *frevo* in the narrow streets of the old city, brandishing parasols to maintain their balance. This traditional carnival, without electric instruments or frequent samba lines, is one of the characteristics of the culture in the state of Pernambuco that is so distinctive and endearing.

As with the state of Bahia, the state of Pernambuco is part of the Nordeste, a territory three times the size of France, characterized by a history, geography, culture, and even an accent that are different from the rest of Brazil.

1/2/3
These rows of small Pernambuco houses in Tracunhaém, Paudalho, and Vitoria de Santo Antao, respectively, show how much residents feel the need to strongly personalize the facade of their homes with color.

4
In Condado, within Pernambuco, the owner of these small residences, influenced by the color scheme in the port of Recife, has created his own interpretation of it here.

1

2

3

4

1 / 2 / 3 / 4
OPPOSITE 1 / 2
The homes in Pernambuco do not all have such colorful exuberance. Yet whether you are in the city of Olinda or the neighboring villages, strong colors are present everywhere, in every variation of the spectrum, and at every level of contrast (1 Paudalho; 2 / 3 / 4 Olinda; opposite, 1 Paudalho; 2 Aliança).

1

2

The history of Pernambuco was marked in 1537 by the arrival of the Portuguese and by the founding of Olinda as the capital, then, a century later, by the Dutch invasion, which changed the state's cultural, economic, and artistic orientation by expanding Recife at the expense of Olinda. As for the region's economy, it has traditionally been based on sugarcane farming, plantations for which cover the cleared-out former tropical forest. Between the *sertão* (a vast, arid steppe) and the sugarcane plantations, there is a transitional zone dedicated to raising livestock and harvesting food. Local resources are not sufficient to nourish the population, which tends to migrate toward more favored, southern regions. The people of Pernambuco, of mixed heritage, are witness to the country's history, a history that includes the Indians, the Portuguese, the Dutch, and even the French.

Today, the old city of Olinda, declared a "natural and cultural landmark for humanity" by UNESCO, practically makes up a suburb of the immense urban expanse of the nearby capital, Recife. It occupies such an exceptional site on hills that tumble into the Atlantic Ocean, that, upon seeing its beauty, the region's first Portuguese governor is said to have exclaimed on March 12, 1535: "O linda posição para uma vila!" ("what a marvelous site for a city!"), from which we get the name Olinda.

3

3
Colors of the national flag, emblematic colors: this is how José Wilso Azevedo celebrated the World Cup, by repainting his house, which had been blue with yellow trim, in green (Pernambuco).

Thanks to livestock, sugarcane, cotton, and the export of Brazilian wood, the standard of living for aristocrats residing in Olinda was quite elevated. They lived on vast manors ruled by luxury and refinement, and prayed in their private chapels, which were magnificently tailored and decorated with an abundance of gold. A deep religious sentiment motivated the city's residents; numerous religious orders—Jesuits, Franciscans, Benedictines, Carmelites—proved quite active in education and cultural affairs, and churches, convents, and monasteries multiplied rapidly. Olinda was an intellectual and artistic center of the highest order during the sixteenth, seventeenth, and eighteenth centuries. The different stages of its history are present in the roadsides lined with beautiful colonial homes and in the public squares decorated with statues and fountains and shaded by characteristically tropical trees. Strolling, one is quickly overcome by the specific charm that radiates from these places so laden with history and by the slightly melancholy atmosphere that reigns there.

1

1
This "window and door" house, located in Condado in the Recife region, is a significant testimony to how architecture can be imagined without an architect, improvised either by the local mason or by the owner himself. Openings and design are emphasized in the contrast in quality between the greens.

1 / 2 / 3 / 4
As discussed in Anna Mariani's book on popular habitats in the Nordeste region (Facades: maisons populaires du Nordeste), *these homes in Pernambuco sometimes show an energetic creativity in the cut of their pediments and the design of decorative patterns, whose inspirations remain unclear. The tonalities are strong but limited in number* (1 *Saint Amaro;* 2 / 3 / 4 *Cachoeira*).

1 / 2 / 3 / 4
These four small homes in the old quarter of Condado are typical of basic, traditional dwellings: they are constructed in taipa de sopapo, a process whereby damp clay is molded onto a skeleton of branches.

Applied to the soil walls, successive layers of limewater paints give the structure a very particular relief within the whole range of pastels.

1

2

3

4

One of the largest urban centers in Brazil, Recife stretches out only a few miles away from the small, colonial city. Recife became the capital of the state of Permanbuco when sugar producers settled it in the seventeenth century, stripping Olinda of its economic superiority, then of its political power.

The city, which takes its name from the coral reefs on which the waves break, is situated at the confluence of the Capiberibe and Beberibe Rivers, on islands and peninsulas connected by bridges. What was originally a vast swampland, cleaned out for the most part by the Dutch, still falls prey to water during heavy floods, and the sea is eating away at the coastline covered in ultramodern apartment buildings.

For the past couple of years, the old section of the port has been the focus of a vast restoration initiative. During our stay in Pernambuco, we met the architect Mõnica Vasconcelos, who was responsible for the coloration design of one part of the neighborhood. The project, initiated by the town hall, intended to return attention to a very interesting, but completely neglected, architectural heritage. Mõnica Vasconcelos believes in the principle that traditional, colonial Portuguese architecture is painted in three colors: a first color for the walls, a second for wood trim, and a third for cornices and various architectural ornamentation; she has added muted tones to the spectrum in order to outline the ornamental details, which differ from one facade to the next.

The recoloring of Recife's old port district, begun in 1993, creates a certain fascination among neighboring villages and towns who make more or less successful interpretations of it, as we discovered in the little town of Goiana. All of the working-class homes on Rua Marchado were freshly repainted in very strong colors—two colors per home—according to a governing coloration outline prescribed by a landscape architect. Another example of the restoration's chromatic influence is in Condado, where Ismaël Gayaō covered the rows of its small rental home facades in bright colors. Here and there, color gives these modest homes what we call an "appeal value."

1

2

3

4

1 / 2 / 3
We came upon Tracunhaem and the colored houses of Paudalho completely by chance. The proliferation of colors and the creativity of contrasts persuaded us to undertake a site analysis.

Creuza Gonçalvès Da Silva, the owner of the currant-colored home, informed us that she repaints her house every year before Christmas, changing color in accordance with her inspiration.

4
This small home in Santo Amaro in the state of Bahia reflects the imaginative angles and patterns that were dear to the residents in the Nordeste region.

The basic rural home has one door and a single window that looks out onto the street (it is called "uma casa e uma janela"). It is constructed either of *taipa pisada*, in other words adobe, with soil filling in wood molds, or by *taipa de sopapo*, a process by which pre-moistened soil is sculpted into balls and thrown onto a framework of branches tied together with thread. The walls are then covered with an earthen surfacing material. A thatched roof and one single room that opens onto a courtyard where cooking and washing are done serves the basic dwelling. Lime paint, regularly touched up, blurs the angles and give the walls a soft luminescence.

In constructions that are more elaborate, more solid, and more costly, walls are made of hollow bricks or cinder blocks and roofs are made of machine-made tiles; one level separates living quarters and sleeping quarters. A decorated veranda with elaborate grating runs along the front of the house; this grating has become a symbol of social status, and is more and more frequently adopted by the more modest classes who wish to identify with the upper classes of society.

This is where color comes into play: sober limewater tones in pastel blue, yellow, pink, and green on the oldest homes of traditional villages, bright and contrasting tones for modern paints. Brazilians love color, but in a certain milieu, one fears making a *brega*, that is to say, something construed as lacking good taste. In this case, discreet harmonies are adopted, with attention paid to tonal grouping. The working classes, on the other hand, happily choose strong, hardy colors in line with their tastes and disposition. Homes are repainted every year in time for Christmas festivities (during the dry season when it is not so hot) and each year colors are changed. The color of a house can be symbolic. For example, in Paudalho, José Wilso Azevedo, who had a blue facade with yellow trim, repainted it green to celebrate the World Cup soccer tournament in his own way—an emblematic color, green is the color of the national flag. In Aliança, a group of highly contrasted red and green houses mark the entrance to the "warm" neighborhood of the little town.

1

The charm of the small homes in Pernambuco does not come solely from the chromatic palette of exteriors—as original and eccentric as it may be—but also from architectural details that personalize each of them and differentiate them from neighboring residences. The innumerable geometric cuts and decorative patterns belie a free and spontaneous creativity endlessly practiced with the greatest simplicity.

Let us agree with Jean Baudrillard, who saw in this folk architecture "a pure object, born at the crossroads of the graphic expression and luminous spontaneity of the Nordeste people, with their denuding and misery . . . a misery that doesn't express itself as misery, but as a wealth of lines and appearances." [1]

1
This color analysis of facades performed in Paudalho on February 16, 1998 shows the diversity in tonality and saturation of the colors chosen by the inhabitants of this small village of Pernambuco. In an important proportion, the dark tonalities are dominated by vermilion, cobalt violet, and marine blue, colors that characterize the originality of the inhabitants' choice. Sometimes, very modest in their architectural language, these houses are often enhanced by elements of detail—bands, frames, and molding—whose colored ornament is an essential personal element.

1. In Anna Mariani, *Facades: maisons populaires du Nordeste*. Rio de Janeiro: Editora Nova Fronteira SA, 1988.

OPPOSITE 1
These watercolors illustrate a few examples of coloration on Nordeste's common dwellings. With their cornices, certain homes recall Portuguese colonial architecture; the other facades compete creatively with the cut of their rooftops, their decorative ornamentation, and chromatic palettes that are as varied as they are inventive.

1

OURO PRETO

After sugarcane, it was the discovery of gold that established Brazil's wealth in the beginning of the eighteenth century. During this period, the city of Ouro Preto (Black Gold) appeared, in the central, mountainous region that took the name Minas Gerais, the province of general mining. The city was reborn in 1720 under the name Vila Rica; at that time, it was just a village consisting of cob and wood houses, to which stone constructions were added starting in 1740.

Ouro Preto and the other cities of Minas Gerais seem very different from Brazilian cities; their picturesque quality reminds one more of the ambiance of certain Portuguese cities.

2

3

1/2
The former capital of Minas Gerais, Ouro Preto, built into steep mountain slopes, is a veritable museum-city. Its slanting streets are lined with old homes from the eighteenth century, carefully repainted in white or pastels.

The assertive tones of the doors and windows contrast strongly with the light tones of the facades.

3
In simple fashion this synthesis chart exhibits the dominant chromatics for dwellings within the center of Ouro Preto, which was analyzed in 1979. The terra-cotta roofs present various shades of brown and ochre.

The sobriety of the exterior palette is vigorously sharpened by elements of the selective palette, where foundations are quite evident. The sash windows are generally painted white.

In Ouro Preto, architectural originality and homogeneity mold themselves to the geographic and socio-cultural condition of each settlement. An economic system relying on slaves for the extraction of gold, rough natural surroundings and transportation difficulties necessitated the use of local building materials.

Unlike the northeastern cities that were built into the existing terrain, the cities of Minas were the focus of urban planning that governed the width of streets, the height of houses, as well as the construction of bridges and fountains that bring water to every neighborhood in the city.

In the case of Ouro Preto, which was established on the steep mountain slopes, the regulations posed a couple of problems. Some streets scale the steepest slopes (these are the *laderas*), while others hug the level curves and are on less of a slope. These streets have often retained their original paving, made of quartzite gravel called *Pé de Moleque*, or Hobo foot,[1] sometimes with a band of large paving stones in the center of schist or quartzite.

The homes that provide shelter for the middle class are low with gently sloping roofs, covered with round tiles in mixed tones ranging from browns and orange-reds.

Most of these residences are built of adobe, a raw clay brick dried in the sun, and the walls have a

1. From the thesis by Yves Leloup, *Les villes du Minas Gerais*. Paris IV, 1969.

coat of limewater. The dominant tone for facades is white, but there are also pastel tints: ochre, pink, light turquoise, and tinted gray. Stone construction is rare.

The most characteristic type of colonial mining home is represented by the *sobrados*, the one- or two-story houses of prominent locals. Despite the presence of lime-based and oxide-based pastels, white is still the color that dominates. Besides, generally speaking, it is a tradition in Brazil to whitewash exteriors in lime, according to several testimonies dating from last century that focus just as much on Minas Gerais as Pernambuco or São Paulo. Back then, whitewashing was achieved with a coating made of shell, stone, or *tabatinga* (white clay).

1

1
As in the other cities of Minas Gerais, Ouro Preto was the subject of an urban planning project concerned with street widths and house heights. This bird's-eye view over the gently inclined rooftops, covered in round tiles, reveals a whole range of terra-cotta browns and orangey reds.

1

2

As for civil and religious buildings, these were constructed by the residents of the mining provinces with financial support from the monarchy. The king of Portugal, seeking to control gold shipments, forbade the construction of religious orders and severely limited communication with the outside world. This situation helped spread an intense and unique artistic and cultural life. As such, the architecture of Ouro Preto, even though it is representative of the Baroque style, was the fruit of a unique and creative interpretation of this style, by local artists and artisans; the design layout, the reduced decoration, and the pursuit of detail refinement give the architecture of this city a fine elegance.

Since 1938, the whole city has been classified as a national monument and the Ministry of Culture has made a considerable effort to restore rundown buildings. The most impressive church is without a doubt São Francisco de Assis, completed in 1810; above the steatite doorway, a medallion crowned with a spiral gable depicts Saint Francis receiving Christ's stigmata. It is the masterpiece of Antonio Francisco Lisboa, the ingenious sculptor nicknamed "Aleijadinho," the little cripple, because of his handicap.

In the selective palette of the habitat, framework has a great visual importance for the whole of the exterior since it strongly highlights the square, double-hung windows. They are sometimes left in natural stone, whose ochre tint contrasts strikingly with the white facade, but, most often, they are painted, whether in a dark monotone pink against a light pink background, dark blue against a light blue background, or in contrasting colors—blue, brown, gray, and sometimes green—against the white facade; we noticed that framework color often differs from one floor to another.

3

1 / 2 / 3
The various cuts around window openings are always underscored with a wide band of color, emphasizing the facade's rhythm and moldings.

1

Horizontal and vertical bands also outline the facade's molding; they are generally the same color as the framework.

Doors are most often in the same tonalities as the bands and framework. This is likewise the case for windows if they are not white; there is a strong prevalence of the range of blues, followed by greens. On the sobrados, windows are adorned with wrought-iron balconies.

As for the foundations, they present an important color surface, due to the uneven terrain; they are painted in neutral colors of gray and medium brown.

The architectural body of dwellings in Ouro Preto, strongly impacted by the natural inclines and by the baroque flourishes on exterior moldings, is rendered even more expressive by the avowed use of tonalities that accentuate detail elements.

1
Ground treatment in the large square, with its even paving stones, recalls the importance of this element within the global perception of an urban environment. Here, the white facades and the dark tones around openings create an asserted contrast, personalizing Ouro Preto's architectural language.

2
In this street, with its slope underscored by the foundations, the facades line up in melodious and contrasting tones, reminding us of Brazilians' love of color.

2

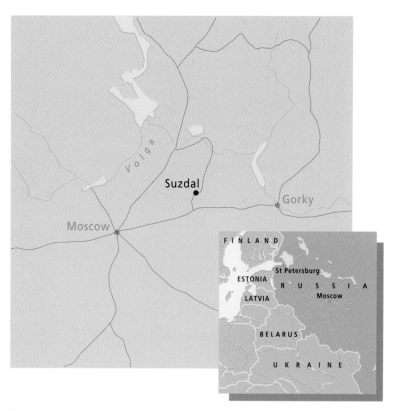

RUSSIA

SUZDAL

Suzdal, northeast of Moscow, is one of the ancient cities whose current configuration was largely drawn out as early as the twelfth or thirteenth century, with the Kremlin and Cathedral of the Nativity on one side of the Kamenka River, and the Saint Dimitri Cathedral on the other side. This was the era when the princes of Suzdal and Vladimir attempted to unify the feudal countryside, but the arrival of the Mongols halted the economic development of Suzdalia.

1

Suzdal, located north of Vladimir, is a small city on a vast farming plain, the Opolie, which once provided grain for Vladimir.

These few homes, in an even line along the street, significantly demonstrate a few characteristics of local color, the yellows, blues, browns, and greens creating the traditional palette's basic vocabulary.

However, in the fourteenth century, the Suzdal princes attempted to reestablish the city's prestige, and the construction of monuments was actively reinitiated, reaching its apogee at the end of the seventeenth century. The numerous churches built in the eighteenth century give an idea of the intense cultural and spiritual development of the period.

In 1788, the city's reconstruction project organized the placement of public squares and main streets, and reserved the town center for residents who could build stone houses, thereby pushing poorer residents into the outlying regions.

Today, with seventy monuments, Suzdal is a museum town where each era has left an architectural and artistic imprint, but where the unity of the whole presides, assisted by the passing of time and by the will of the people to faithfully preserve the inheritance bestowed by prior generations.

1

1

This view, encompassing the whole of the Intercession-of-the-Virgin monastery, gives an idea of the extent and richness of religious buildings, which were constructed in large numbers in Suzdal, mainly between the sixteenth and eighteenth centuries.

Brick is the dominant building material here; it is generally coated in limewater, which in winter blends harmoniously into the snowy landscape. In the foreground, the Kamenka River drifts peacefully by.

Our site study, undertaken in May 1990, looked at an ensemble of small, wooden peasant houses, called *isbas*, remarkable for the quality of their architecture and the richness of their chromatic harmony.

Wooden architecture is one of the representative attributes of Russian culture. It is with wood that Russians not only constructed their residences but also their churches and cathedrals, and wooden architecture has widely influenced stone architecture, notably in the seventeenth and eighteenth centuries, when small wooden churches that had fallen victim to fires were progressively replaced by stone churches. At the beginning of the twentieth century, wooden architecture was still widely predominant, not only in the countryside, but also in cities, where it exhibited the same characteristics as the traditional isba.

The isba has always been the focus of great care on the part of Russian peasants, who demonstrated and still demonstrate all their skill, together with a clear artistic sense, during construction. Conceived in the forest where Russian civilization first developed, the isba displays in its external character a number of characteristic traits that have evolved relatively little since its description in 1847 by the baron of Haxthausen in his "Studies on the Interiors of Russia," a description cited in an excellent work by B. Kerblay on the Russian isba: "The lateral side of the houses, which alone is decorated, faces the street and has no door . . . The main room of the habitation, ordinarily lit by three windows, occupies the whole side facing the street. Above, there is sometimes a small bedroom with a window opening onto the balcony; it usually serves as a bedroom for young girls and figures endlessly in folk songs, under the term *terema*, as a place of mystery and poetry . . . Only rich peasants paint the exterior of their house; the colors they favor are green for the walls and red for the roof."[1]

Certain isbas date from the end of the nineteenth century, but generally they do not last more than about fifty years due to the nature of the materials.

1

1

This close-up of a door's details articulates the texture of the wood, used for traditional isbas, as well as the characteristic colors of the protective paint.

1. Basile H. Kerblay, *L'Isba d'hier et d'aujourd'hui*. Lausanne: L'Age d'Homme, 1973.

1

2

3

4

1 / 2 / 3 / 4
These four isbas in Suzdal and its surrounding areas highlight the dominant traits of this region's popular architecture: the gable with its three windows faces the street with a detailed facade whose wooden friezes and framework often create veritable decorative lace.

1

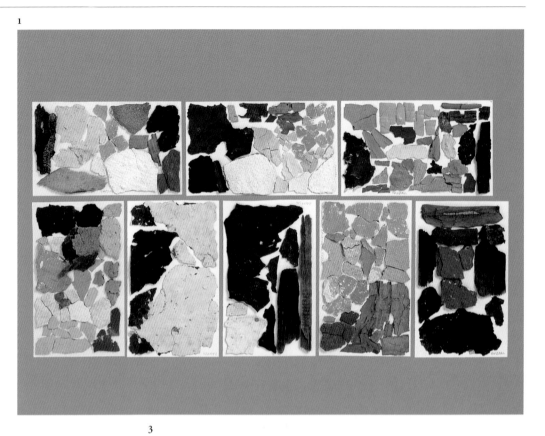

1

Collected in Suzdal and Zagorsk, these material samples are primary and valuable witnesses to the color and substance of various components of local architecture: wood, brick, coating, and paint. Whatever their substance and texture, each material is a constituent element in the site's true palette.

2

3

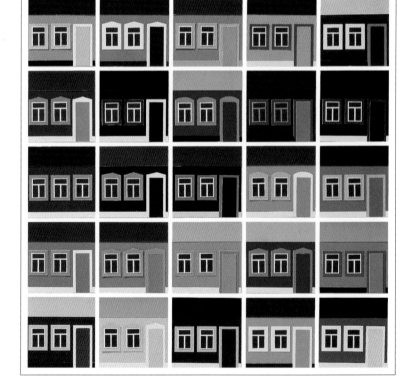

2/3

These two synthesis charts, completed in Suzdal in May 1990, eloquently illustrate the chromatic physiology of this small city's traditional habitat, which is both diversified and homogeneous in its architectural and chromatic expression.

The walnut or gray color of painted sheet-metal roofs is a constant within the general palette. Framework and windows, painted in white or in contrasting tones, are essential elements of the selective palette.

Russian homes are made of wood—conifer, alder, birch, and sometimes oak—only foundations are made of stone and brick to protect against humidity. They are easy to erect and it is an opportunity for the joyous reunion of family, relatives, and friends. The log structure is sometimes left bare, sometimes covered with planks. When the *srub*, or wooden cage, is finished, which takes one day, it is the carpenter's turn to get involved in order to position the roof, doors, and windows.

For a long time, the two-sloped roof was thatched or laid with planks. This type of dwelling offers the advantage of being easily taken apart, and Russians move with their home, which they then transport to their new place of residence.

1

This house, drawn on May 27, 1990, in the village of Kidekcha, a few miles from Suzdal, displays the characteristic traits of the isbas of central Russia.

Color pencils are an excellent and practical way to catalog the different tones that make up the palette of a structure and its surroundings.

1

Today, builders still frequently use the same materials and techniques of the past for the construction of homes (the most notable difference consists in the use of sheet metal, tile, and tarred shingles for the roof). This reverence for the use of traditional materials and techniques bestows a great visual unity upon the Russian village. It is the décor—sculpted or painted—that distinguishes one home from its neighbor. Paint plays into the facade and intervenes in elements of the selective palette (door and window frames, cornices, sculpted wood pediments) with solid-color contrasts that introduce white, blue, red, green, and yellow. In the province of Moscow, recent constructions are covered in an ochre-colored paint that protects the wood.

1/2/3

OPPOSITE 1

These four homes in Suzdal and its outlying areas seem to testify to the residents' taste for chrome green.

1

2

3

4

1 / 2 / 3 / 4

OPPOSITE 1

The selective palette for isbas in central Russia is not only highlighted by the contrasting colors of the facade's painted planks, it comprises a very personal ornamentation for the house.

The artisan's creativity and imagination come through in the detailed cuts of the wooden frames and pediments.

1

The isba seen in Suzdal displays certain architectural characteristics, such as the *podklet*, a finished basement designed, in this region, for storing potatoes. The roof of galvanized sheet metal is painted reddish-brown, green, or ochre.

The sculpted décor is enriched with animal and plant motifs that are valued in Vladimiro-Suzdalian religious architecture, notably owing to the talent of former shipbuilders on the Volga after the arrival of the steamboat.

Windows framed in sculpted wood are particularly elaborate and often take on the appearance of finely worked lace accentuated with white, with blue frequently added as a counterpoint.

1

1
The framework of the isba, composed of logs, may be left visible, as is the case here; this calls to mind traditional Scandinavian and Canadian homes, as well as the elevated chalets in the Alps.

Freshly repainted in blue and brown, the general palette is supported by petrol-blue windows accentuated in white.

Blue is a hue that is particularly appreciated by the inhabitants of Suzdal. Andrei Efimov, a member of the Academy of Architecture in Moscow, who participated amiably in our site study, emphasizes in reference to this: "The need for a more complex colored environment is satisfied today in part by painting walls and exterior house details in blue, from cobalt to lapis. The reason for this color innovation was the appearance of blue paint on storefronts in Suzdal. I overheard a resident from a village near Moscow asking his neighbor who was leaving for some shopping in Moscow: 'Buy me some paint for the house. What color? Blue, of course, you know how beautiful it is.'"

1/2
Here, again, blue is the prevalent color. Ever since it arrived in the city's stores, the residents have been virtually infatuated with this color. The contrasting whites and browns emphasize the details of the selective palette.

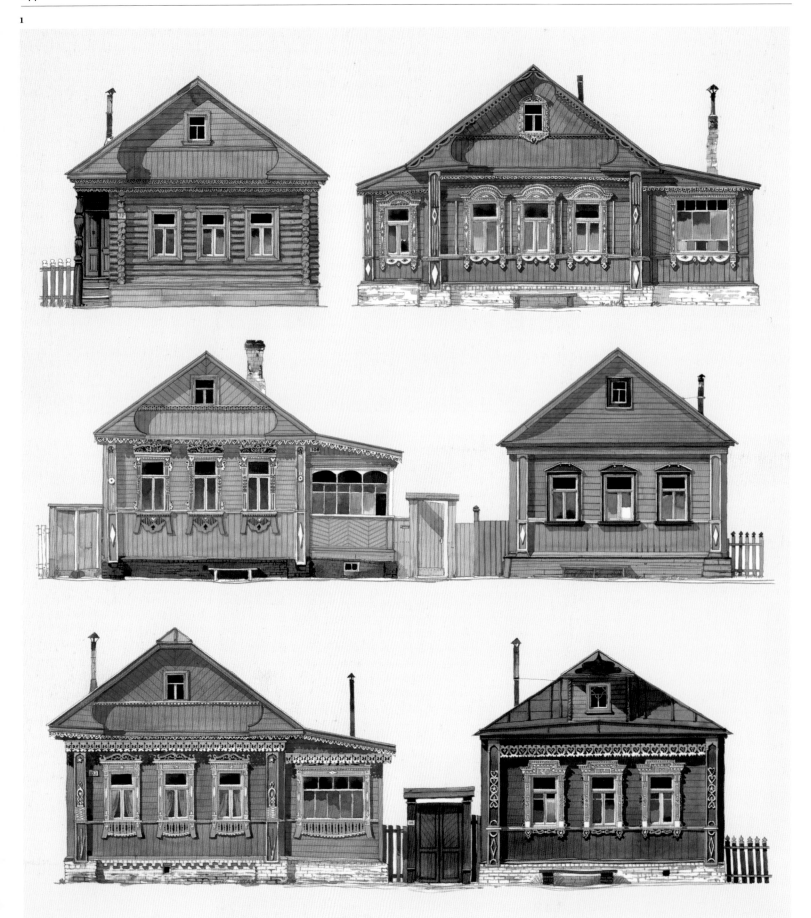

1

2

3

4

OPPOSITE 1
Suzdal's isbas, whether made of logs or planks, are based on the same architectural model with three ground-floor windows decorated with more or less detailed wood carvings.

Most often, the wood is protected by a solid-colored paint, which contrasts with the elements of the selective palette.

1 / 2 / 3 / 4
The roofs often incorporate painted sheet metal, colored mainly in gray, green, and red oxides.

Carefully painted, wooden garden fences contribute to the refinement and charm of this home, as poetic as it is colorful.

SOUTH AFRICA

South of the Tropic of Capricorn, South Africa comprises a vast geographic ensemble that is relatively unpopulated, principally due to the infertility of the majority of land. The first occupants of this country were the Bushmen, a hunting community, then the Hottentots, who were nomads. Colonization began in the middle of the seventeenth century, with the Dutch arriving on the Cape and installing a post to provision the East India Company. When the colonists proceeded toward the country's northern regions, they came upon the Bantu who, coming from central Africa, were heading south.

1

1

1
OPPOSITE 1
Crossing the Gauteng (formerly, the Transvaal) and Free State provinces toward the Lesotho region, here and there you come upon a popular habitat where exterior design is still elemental, often well hidden among the grazing and farming lands. Two tribes in particular distinguish themselves with their lively traditions of geometric and figurative patterns, with color playing an essential role: the Sotho and Ndebele (1 residence of the Ndebele king in Weltevrede, in Gauteng; opposite, 1 Clarens in the Free State).

1

THE SOTHO

The Sotho and Nguni, from whom the Ndebele descend, belong to a group of southern Bantu, established in Africa at least two centuries prior to the arrival of the first Dutch colonists at the Cape in 1662.

Just as the Nguni branch split into different nations—the Swazi, Zulu, and Ndebele on one side, the Xhosa, Thembu, and Mpondo on the other—the Sotho branch also diversified into the Tswana, Pedi, Venda, and Sotho.

Faced with the advance of Dutch settlers who sought the best lands for establishing farms, the Bantu herding-farming tribes began to organize under the authority of their patriarchs. This is how

the Zulu, Matabele, Swazi, and Sotho military regimes were formed. This last group fought against the Boer invasion until their defeat in 1867, and would have become extinct if the English had not declared Basutoland, the Sotho territory, a British colony. This is the modern-day state of Lesotho, which forms a veritable enclave within the Republic of South Africa. It is there, and in neighboring regions, that the southern Sotho live; it is their habitat that we studied.

Lesotho is a small, mountainous territory about the size of Belgium. Mainly devoted to agriculture and livestock, it had until recently quite meager resources—the essential resources coming from the men's work in the mines of South Africa—which kept this state dependent upon its powerful neighbor. A decisive turning point came a few years

ago, thanks to the establishment of numerous South African firms which found in Lesotho a cheap workforce. In addition, the Maloti Mountains, which reach altitudes of 9,842 feet (3,000 meters) in spots, are currently the stage for massive work sites, such as the LHWP (Lesotho Highlands Water Project). The water that accumulates in an immense reservoir constructed on the Orange River feeds into the Ash River and rejoins the arid plateaus of the Johannesburg area. Thanks to these mountains, Lesotho is the "water tower" of the vast South African Republic.

1

2

3

4

1 / 2 / 3 / 4

OPPOSITE 1

The Sotho are a remarkably homogeneous people, whether they live in Lesotho or the Free State, and their homes testify to their attachment to ancestral tradition. These small, earthen homes capped with thatched roofs have similar proportions and sizes. Sometimes left in the natural color of the clay masonry, sometimes with a colored clay coating, the exteriors display different types of personalized décor. Here, a white line traces a decorative pattern around the walls; earthen embroidery delicately frames the panels of the facade; and elsewhere still, encrusted stones protect the foundation from rainwater (Butha-Buthe and its outlying areas, Lesotho, Free State).

1

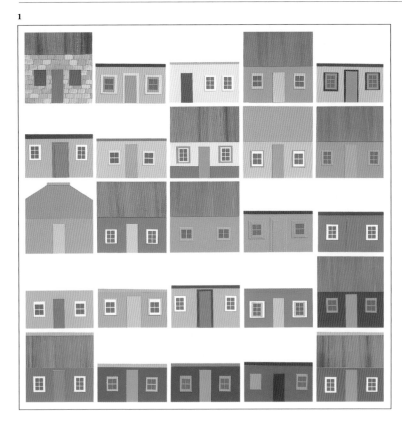

1

These documents, created in April 1997, have to do with the village of Pokani, in the Butha-Buthe region, northeast of Lesotho. Most buildings are covered in corrugated sheet metal; in this case, the facade alone constitutes the dominant palette, which splits into two color families: the tinted grays made with natural pigments and the red and orange tones made from organic pigments. As for the selective palette of the doors, it is mainly divided between balanced blues and greens.

2

3

1

1 / 2

OPPOSITE 2 / 3

When the thatching disintegrates, it is replaced by corrugated sheet metal. The extremely sober facades sometimes forgo all decoration: the smooth, brushed, or scratched texture of the coating thereby reclaims its entire tactile flavor. In the sizzling sunlight, one can see hints of the interlaced branches under the soil coating that form the skeleton of the structure (Free State between Clarens and Bethlehem, Lesotho).

2

1
Celine Hlowane's house, on Stephanium farmland between Clarens and Bethlehem, is a perfect example of traditional Basotho dwellings.

The relief of the decorative pattern and the round angles express the artisan's care and creativity.

1

The Sotho form a largely homogeneous people because of their roots, their attachment to their language and customs, and their relative isolation. These South Africans are proud of their culture, their humanist system of values, and their traditions of eloquence; they all share the same religion, Christianity, which is an additional unifying force.

Southern Sotho homes are generally grouped in hamlets or villages; during periods of uncertainty, these were established preferably on elevated summits in order to help keep an eye on the surrounding regions. The village leader's home occupied the most elevated spot, and, here and there, the homes of the most important community members were erected, the central space reserved for livestock.

The traditional Sotho house consists of a circular earthen hut topped with a cone-shaped thatched roof. This type of dwelling is very popular in Lesotho, but in the Free State, rectangular earthen homes can also be seen. In the mountain regions, stone is also used for hut foundations or even for wall construction. The floor of the hut is coated with a mix of clay and cow dung which is trampled until a smooth, hard surface is obtained, which is then decorated by the women.

Sotho women take an active role in building the house: while men saw wood and erect frames, they cut grass and reeds, make the flooring, and coat the walls. It is also the women who, when necessary, erect the earthen walls that surround the home's courtyard and decorate them. Men and women make clay bricks that are used in the construction of the hut, but it is the men who build the walls.

1

2

3

1 / 2 / 3
*Every possible earthen color is
juxtaposed in colored bands to
underscore the horizontality of rural
habitations.*

154

There is such a strong symbolic connection between women and home that when a Sotho woman dies, they say that her husband's house has crumbled. Women still paint murals on different buildings surrounding the courtyard of the rural home, according to traditions that date back several centuries as archeological research has shown, traditions eventually adopted by the Ndebele people. These paintings, or designs based on molding and engraving, form a kind of prayer to the ancestors, considered to be mediators between humans and the divine. The ceremonies that take place in the sacred space of the courtyard, the prayers, the sacrifices, all seek to call upon the ancestors and to ask their intervention for rain and fertility. A certain type of woman produces this mural art: she is rural and intends to remain faithful to the town, and it is she who guarantees that the traditions will be upheld.

Pictorial forms of expression are slightly different depending on whether you are in Lesotho itself or in the Free State. In Lesotho, there is more decoration made from pebbles that form a sort of simple mosaic, which is more rigid and austere than painted décor and symbolically depicts the surrounding mountain landscape. These compositions, based on pebbles embedded into the earthen walls, exhibit a rather limited range of mineral colors, but their structure enlivens the wall with shadow and light effects that vary throughout the day. Among the usual designs, we noticed a predominance of the four-petal flower motif, a traditional and symbolic motif that tends to be used everywhere. Another type of décor consists of engraving parallel lines along the moist soil of the wall with the help of a fork, comb, or even fingers. In this way, women design veritable landscapes on their walls that celebrate their work in the fields; their emphasis changes with every hour of the day. The backdrop for Sotho décor is in brown, ochre, black, and gray tonalities depending on the nature of the soil used.

In the Free State, if mural art always calls to mind the techniques of engraving, pebble-based mosaic, or even molding, tonalities of painted design, which emphasize relief by subordinating color to sculptural effect, explode on the main facades of traditional round huts or on secondary walls of rectangular homes. In these regions, the Sotho have partially fallen under Ndebele influences; in addition to their soil-based natural pigments, they now have the option of using synthetic pigments as well as geometric designs.

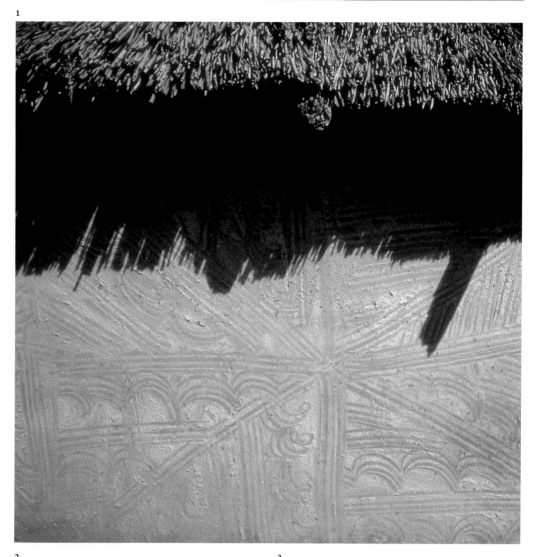

1 / 2 / 3
OPPOSITE 1 / 2 / 3 / 4 / 5
The chromatic character of common homes of the Sotho and Ndebele tribes is not simply limited to form, color, and décor; it also takes into consideration material and surface textures, with their remarkable refinement and emotion. Numerous are the manual techniques used for delicately treating the surface (Gauteng, Loupoort, Lesotho, Gauteng, Loopspruit, Free State, Clarens region).

In addition to the traditional motifs, the triangle is a figure found all over; it symbolically joins woman and the divine, the Earth and the sky. This reading is reinforced by the use of symbolic colors—black, connected to ancestors and rain-bearing clouds, red, and light ochre extracted from the soil, both of which are used in the women's initiation rites. Triangles lined up side by side form zigzags and often decorate transitional spaces such as openings and corners. Unlike most African tribes that occasionally embellish their facades for a celebration or particular event, the Sotho people, even renovating frequently, will permanently preserve the design on their home, which becomes a sort of visual language that confirms women's primacy over the home, plant life, and land.

2

1

3

4

5

The most splendid examples of this art are not along the highways, but on dirt roads and in the open country among the fields and prairies where farm animals graze.

This ephemeral art, which flourishes on earthen walls, is in danger of extinction as farmers build modern homes for their workers out of cinder blocks and as the countryside loses its population to urban expansion.

1 / 2 / 3 / 4 / 5 / 6 / 7 / 8
While the surface is still freshly coated, patterns ranging from the most simple to the most complex are engraved, often with fingers, sometimes with a fork, creating a geometric or stylistic floral design. In Lesotho, embedded pebbles form a sort of decorative mosaic with earthen tones.

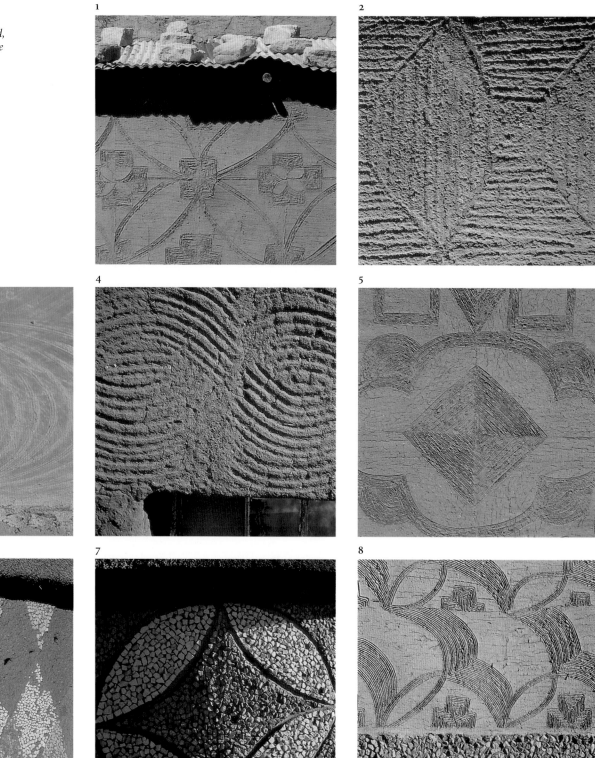

1

2

3

4

5

6

7

8

OPPOSITE 1
These illustrations give an idea of the colors on ordinary Sotho and Ndebele homes. The top two rows focus on the Sotho home with two examples of clay buildings with traditional patterns in ochres and browns, and two examples of more recent cinder block homes whose surfaces and designs rely on organic pigments of strong, contrasting colors. The four homes in the bottom two rows are characteristic of Ndebele habitats and mural patterns with, on the one hand, patterns and mineral pigments from former times, and on the other, more modern designs made with industrial paints.

1

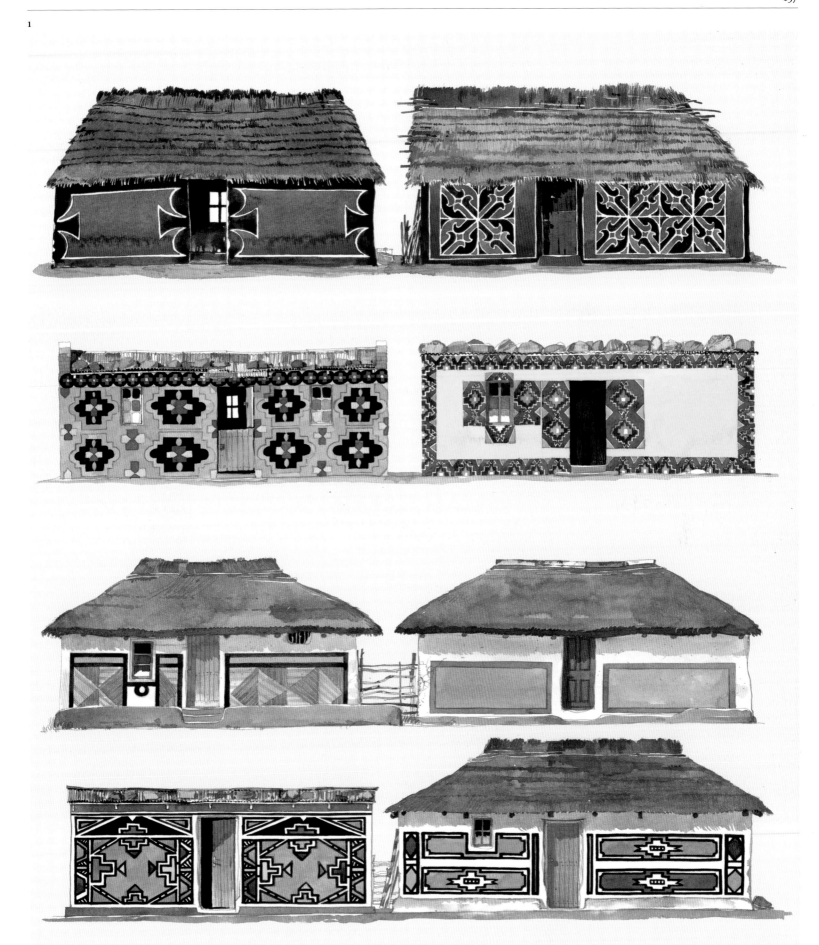

THE NDEBELE

The Ndebele, whose roots are mixed with those of the Nguni, separated into two branches in the seventeenth century: the northern Ndebele who merged with the Sotho-Tswana, and the southern Ndebele. The latter is further subdivided into two groups: the Nzundza who, with exceptional tenacity, have maintained their language and customs against the forces of change.

The Ndzundza, for their part, have preserved an avowed cultural identity, thanks no doubt to having had to fight bitterly for survival. In fact, the Boers of the ZAR (Zuid Afrikaanse Republik) initiated a merciless war in 1882 against the Ndebele, who, under the leadership of king Mabhogo, comprised one of the most powerful tribal groups in the north of the country. Vanquished, the Ndebele were practically reduced to servitude by the Boers, at least for the five years they were forced to work on the colonist's farms. At the end of the five years, some had to leave the farm straightaway, without money, and led nomadic lives, picking up work here and there. Still others were not liberated by their masters at the prescribed time, and were without legal recourse. Others still, who received better treatment, or who did not know where to go, stayed on the farms of their own accord. Finally, in the beginning of the 1970s, the government established a national homeland for the Ndebele in the KwaNdebele area of northeastern Pretoria. This brought an end to the years of wandering and servitude.

During these trying years, the imprisoned king of the Ndebele never stopped encouraging the members of his tribe to maintain the language and observe tradition. In 1968, David Mabusa Mapoch was officially declared king of the Ndebele by the South African government; his palace, decorated by his half-sister, Francine Ndimande, is located in KwaNdebele. In the national homeland, living conditions are rough because there are no local industries and the residents, mainly men, travel two to eight hours a day by bus in order to work in the city. Certain tribal members prefer to remain on the farms, others reside in the industrial zone of Bronkhorstspruit in eastern Pretoria, in the Wildt district northwest of the administrative capital, or even in the Nebo district.

1

1
In the suburbs of Clarens, among recent cinder block constructions, this house painted by Anna Makoena, age 21, is distinctive in its exuberant colors and design. The principal pattern of stylized flowers acts as both a symbol and signal (Free State).

1

1

Black, yellow, white, brown: such is the chromatic range for Julia Mputi's house. It is admirable for its sobriety of composition, the forceful expression of the pattern, and the rigorously contrasting colors. Outlining windows with diamonds is pretty common among the Sotho.

2

For the Sotho, mural design is an art that has been passed on by women from generation to generation. Older patterns with earthen colors are a type of prayer, asking the spirits of ancestors to bring rain and fertility (near Clarens, Free State).

2

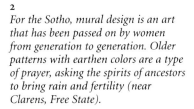

1/2
On Paul Farrel's farm and in Stephanium, the clusters of farm workers' homes display the bright, explosive colors of modern organic pigments, which contrast strongly with the sobriety of traditional mineral pigments (Free State).

1

If the South Ndebele have survived as a nation, it is thanks to their faithfulness to customs and beliefs. In particular, they believe that their ancestors want their sites as well as their traditions to be maintained, both of which are taught to young boys during their initiation period in the hills and to young girls during their time at home.

The Ndebele home borrows a lot from the Sotho home: a blend of soil and cow dung is applied to circular piles of soil; the Ndebele construct rectangular homes, often covered with thatching, but more often with corrugated sheet metal. There are still traditional round huts to be found here and there. For the Ndebele, it is the individual home, or the ensemble of huts and homes that belong to one family, that prevails. This grouping, located a certain distance from the nearest neighbor, is inhabited by a man, his wife, or wives, their sons and, when necessary, unmarried daughters. The huts are organized according to a well-defined, traditional design—the central hut belongs to the wife of the family head and all of the huts' doors face the space reserved for livestock.

Through Sotho influences, the Ndebele began to trace patterns with their fingers on the still-moist clay walls of their houses but adopted an original design style with geometric lines. In their eyes, this decorative practice has a sacred quality, guaranteeing the continuity of tradition so desired by their ancestors. The colors used come from the earth—brown, ochre, yellow, gray—as well as pink and mauve from crushed rocks, white from limewater, and black from charcoal. There are symbolic colors: red ochre extracted from the soil represents communication with ancestors' spirits, the white that frames the doors and windows wards off evil spirits. Sometimes women walk great distances in order to locate the colored soil they need; in this way, they have a lifetime reserve of pigment. In fact, for the Ndebele and for the Sotho, women are sovereign in the house; they participate in its construction, actively maintain it, decorate, and paint it. And when a Ndebele woman dies, her house is abandoned and returns to the land from which it came.

2

1

2

3

4

1 / 2 / 3 / 4
Paul Farrel's vast farm is home to a veritable village where the numerous farmhands own either an earthen home or a more recently constructed cinder block house. Cans of paint were given to them so they could paint their houses as they wished, both inside and out. The result is a visible testament to authentic, popular mural art that is far from certain tourist misconceptions (Free State).

1

2

3

4

1

1

OPPOSITE 1 / 2 / 3 / 4
Industrial paints allow for a greater range of expressive freedom in tone and contrast. With this new vocabulary comes graphic and pictorial creativity for the designs produced by *Sotho women in the Free State. The composition is spread across the whole exterior, utilizing friezes, framework, and central wall sections (Free State).*

1/2

OPPOSITE 1

*North of Pretoria, the village of
Soshanguwe is a squatter camp where
members from four tribes come
randomly and temporarily to set up
home; among these are the Sotho and
Nguni, neither of whom has received a
fixed territory from the public powers.
Visiting this informal settlement, we
were impressed by the meticulous care
that all the residents give to their
private space. With found materials,
the residents create simple, well-tended
constructions, reminding us of the
importance South Africans traditionally place on their homes. Here,
however, designs are rare. The
combination of different materials
produces spontaneous and creative
exterior compositions governed by
rhythm, substance, structure, and
color.*

1

Alongside traditional earthen-colored design, there is also a very colorful mural artistry with geometric forms that is considered typically Ndebele. The manner of painting is relatively recent, appearing in the 1940s, seemingly in response to the need or desire to make a clear distinction between them and neighboring tribes. This is what we call color identity. Acrylic paints, available since 1945, are used in conjunction with mineral pigments.

Decorative patterns are often inspired by a given home's architecture, patterns that also figure in work woven with pearls that the Ndebele women make. For Francine Ndimande, one of the most reputable painters along with Esther Mahlangu, the mural art so characteristic of the Ndebele people comes from pearl-weaving in which designs were limited by the choice of colors. The technique they use requires geometry and abstraction that limit the representational possibilities to a combination of verticals, horizontals, and diagonals. However, mural painting is a freer art form than working with pearls, and certain elements of modern city

life, such as telephones and electric light bulbs, elements that the Ndebele lack, are starting to appear.

Some researchers think that it is a question here of a form of symbolic appropriation. For the anthropologist Gary N. van Wyk, it is moreover a question of a form of resistance: "The Ndebele mural tradition, adapted from the Sotho, was consciously promoted to express pride in cultural identity and resistance to colonization."[1] In either case, unlike designs that are scratched onto soil,

1. Gary N. van Wyk in *Courtyard*, Musée Nationale des Arts d'Afrique et d'Océanie et Musée d'Art Moderne de Villeneuve-d'Ascq, 1996.

1

1

OPPOSITE 1 / 2
These two pages show some homes that belong to the Sbanyoni family, about 25 miles (40 kilometers) from Middelburg. Off the beaten path and lost among the grasses, this cluster of thatched, earthen houses is a unique
demonstration, both for its quality and uncommonness, of Ndebele art as it was popularly practiced before organic pigments arrived on the market. The painting is done by the wife of the head of the family (photographed at right), who buys only white and makes the other colors with natural pigments.
The geometric pattern of the court wall is still widely in use, even in more modern contexts (Loupoort).

this mode of expression is first of all purely decorative. A link between tradition and modernity, it is constantly evolving. Unfortunately, such an art risks extinction. The reasons for this vary: today thousands of Ndebele live on the outskirts of KwaNdebele in shanty towns whose corrugated sheet metal shacks do not easily lend themselves to painted décor. Beyond this, a certain number of young boys flee in order to avoid undergoing the initiation ordeal, which has been condemned by the health services and certain intellectuals. In addition, cities are irresistibly drawing in the young, who thereby abandon their customs and forget their ancestors.

1

2

1

2

3

4

1

2

3

4

1/2/3/4
OPPOSITE 1/2/3/4
These are details from foundations and courtyard walls with sober colors made from mixing clay and cow dung, which are engraved with geometric patterns following the traditional ikghuphu process. With parallel lines, they evoke the freshly cut fields and call to mind the close symbolic ties between woman and home, plant, and earth.

1

1 / 2
In this village, the residents are waiting to have sufficient funds to buy the paint needed to renovate designs that have been faded by weather conditions (near Wintervield).

2

1

1
Ndebele mural art is currently regarded as one of the treasures of African art.

Women are the ones who paint the facades and develop patterns that reflect the events that shape both family and village life (Marie Ndimande's house, in Weltevrede).

1

1 / 2

The unique character of Ndebele designs comes mainly from the geometric shapes partitioned in black lines and from the use of bright, contrasting colors, most often against a white background. This style of painting, which dates from the 1940s, is a clear distinction between Sotho and Ndebele art. The acrylic paints with organic pigments have progressively led to a wide range of tones (1 Bronkhorstspruit; 2 Weltevrede).

2

1

2

3

4

1 / 2 / 3 / 4
Barrier walls and gates receive as much careful attention as facades, showing the importance given to courtyards, which are traditionally considered sacred spaces (1 Francine Ndimande's house in Weltevrede;

2 Loopspruit; 3 Weltevrede; 4 Esther Mahlangu's house, Weltevrede).

1

2

3

4

1

1/2

OPPOSITE 1/2/3/4
Ndebele decorative patterns, painted by women, are generally geometric and contain stylized figurative symbols. Traditional symbols deal with the home and natural elements, but these are often accompanied by patterns that evoke the West and modern conveniences such as planes, electric light bulbs, and razors (Weltevrede and surrounding areas).

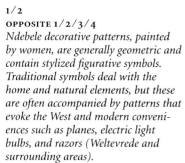

2

1

ALGERIA

GHARDAIA AND M'ZAB

The history of Ibadites settling into this region of the Algerian Sahara is closely related to the religious choices of a small Muslim sect that makes up one branch of Kharidjism, the oldest schism in Islam.

In the beginning of the tenth century, after the destruction of the Tahert kingdom founded in Algeria by the imam Ibn Rostem and the people's subsequent withdrawal to Sedrata in the Sahara, from where they were expelled a century and a half later, the Ibadites finally found secure shelter in the pebbly M'zab desert. They settled around the Oued M'zab, or M'zab River, in the heart of the Chebka region (in Arabic, lace or net), a limestone plateau criss-crossed by a complex network of oueds that form deep valleys, from which it takes its name.

The oueds that cross the gray and black rock are arid, except during the annual rain, and are only recognizable by their sand beds. They feed into a deep underground bed of groundwater from where the Ibadites have for a long time obtained the water necessary for consumption and farm irrigation, at a high labor cost, with the help of a pulley and yoked animals. Since 1938, automation has spread, thanks to semi-artesian drilling. Palm groves offer the three levels of vegetation found in Saharan oases: under palm trees, in irrigated gardens, lush plants such as vegetables, grains, and fruit trees grow; but this is not sufficient for local consumption. Raising livestock is rarely practiced by Mozabites; only nomads own camel and ovine herds.

1

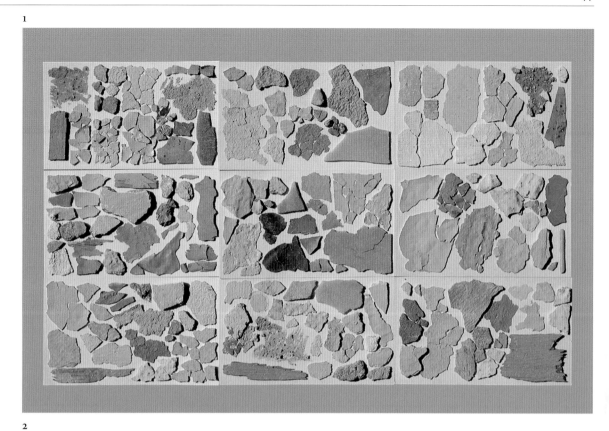

1 / 2

OPPOSITE 1

These sketches, made in Ghardaïa in April 1984, present a subjective interpretation of each site's chromatic atmosphere. Samplings of exterior surfaces and framework paints round out the process by supplying authentic, objective elements. The photo provides an overall view and reveals the components of the urban weave: proportion, rhythm, material, and color.

2

The population of M'zab is mainly composed of Ibadites of Berber origin and foreigners who have converted to Ibadism, but Malekites, who belong to a different ethnic group, make up about 40 percent; the latter tend to work in jobs related to agriculture and construction. Mozabite society is governed by lay and religious institutions. Among the lay institutions, the "fraction," or basic administrative unit, regroups families having a common ancestor. Each fraction, directed by a council, chooses to be a part of either one of the two çoffs, or political parties: the Chergui çoff (eastern clan) and the Gherbi çoff (western clan). The winning çoff participates in the executive functions of the Djemaa, or assembly of elders. Since Algerian liberation, the cities of M'zab have reunited into a single commune where each one has its representatives.

Religious structures have maintained their importance: the tolba, or clerics, the spiritual elite of those who have completed advanced studies in the Koranic sciences, and their representatives, under the direction of the imam, hold the reins of knowledge, morality, justice, and religion. Furthermore, a very conservative assembly of women jealously keeps watch for the unfailing respect of traditions and morality.

For centuries, the different orders that govern Mozabite society have been able to maintain ancestral values to which the Ibadite community is deeply attached and have thus guaranteed their survival. For the past few years however, an evolution has been brewing under the influence of modern ideas circulated, in particular, by radio and television. Women who until now, along with the clerics, were the guardians of tradition, have begun to move around by automobile and leave the valley in order to follow their husbands. But in 1984, during our study in Ghardaïa, women made their way in the street, always covered in a thick veil of white wool that hides almost their entire face, leaving only one eye visible.

1

1

This panoramic view across Ghardaïa reveals the coherence of a traditional Mozabite habitat made rhythmic by the horizontality of its roof-terraces. The city is organized in concentric streets around the central mosque topped by a minaret. The dominant color for this general palette is an ochre sand tone punctuated by white, blue, and green washes.

1 / 2 / 3

The souk in Ghardaïa is an open square surrounded on all four sides by arcades where shops are located. This wide space, laid out like a pattern, creates a breathing space in an urban environment that is otherwise quite dense. Whitewashed in the past with limewater, this public square was just repainted in sand tones during our study, in 1984.

1

2

3

For centuries, the essential M'zab resources have come from the temporary emigration of Mozabites, especially in Tell where they practice profitable commercial activities, mainly in specialty foods. These are informed businessmen with proverbial skillfulness who invest all of their profits in palm groves or in buying apartment buildings. The discovery of oil and the industrialization of the Sahara have once again spurred economic activity in the valley and have had inevitable repercussions on the inhabitants' living conditions and on the evolution of the way of thinking.

The M'zab valley includes five fortified cities, *ksour* in Arabic, which maintained their autonomy until Algerian independence. They were constructed successively from 1011 to 1347, the first one being El Atteuf (The Bend), so called because it is situated on a hill in a bend in the oued. As in all Ibadite cities, the ramparts were built first, then the mosque, before residences. It is the only city in M'zab with two mosques, perhaps witnesses to internal fighting. The ksar is completely surrounded with cemeteries, vast lands littered with pottery shards and objects that belonged to the deceased so that families can recognize the plot attributed to them. The most important cemetery has a mosque, Sidi Brahim, an important place of pilgrimage that is said to have inspired Le Corbusier for his chapel in Ronchamp.

When the ramparts of El Ateuf became filled with residents, a group of Ibadites led by a sheik then founded a second ksar, independent of the first, called Bou Noura (The Bright One), built on a rock at the convergence of two oueds. The small city is protected on its lower side by rampart-houses, the mosque itself forming a rampart; the upper part is practically in ruins. As for the bazaar, at the eastern extremity it has a purely local usage in this city that is relatively poor in relation to the rest of this "pentapolis."

1

1

OPPOSITE 1 / 2 / 3 / 4
*Streets in Mozabite cities are narrow,
and yet surprisingly luminous under
the intense rays of sunlight in this
region of the Sahara. The light
reflecting off the vertical walls and
ground irradiates the space and lends*

*a particular feel to the colors of the
tiny streets (1 Beni-Isguen; opposite,
1 / 3 / 4 Beni-Isguen; 2 Ghardaïa).*

1

2

3

4

Beni-Isguen was then established on the right bank of the M'zab oued, where it flows into the N'Tissa oued. It is the preeminent Holy City (its name means "son of those who hold the law"). There are three religious sites: the former Tafilalt mosque, named for the original old city, the actual mosque with its schools and meeting rooms—the most important in M'zab—and a Boudjira place of prayer, one side of which is open to men, the other to women. The ksar is encircled by high walls and entered through doors that are closed at nightfall. Here the symbol of a particularly rigorous faithfulness to traditional values can be found. The bazaar, triangle-shaped, is a particularly lively place with daily auctions of every possible item, including homes. It is a privileged place of meeting for the city men who sit on stone benches all around the square, until the hour of prayer. The nomads who have come to sell their handcrafted work fill the center of the public square.

Melika (the Queen) was founded, in turn, on the summit of a rocky peak by Beni-Isguen, on the left bank of the M'zab River, halfway between Ghardaïa and Beni-Isguen. It is distinct from the latter in its openness to outsiders, such as the sheik Sidi Aïssa, whose tomb is a place of pilgrimage for the whole confederation. The Ibadite mosque is in the center of this town dominated by a minaret, next to the bazaar, which is exceptional in the M'zab, since markets are traditionally separated from places of worship.

Ghardaïa, the most important and also the most recent city, has lent its name to the entire commune. Unlike the other cities of the pentapolis, it has a vast area within its walls which makes one assume that it was, from its inception, meant to welcome numerous inhabitants. It is worth noting that the ksar developed concentrically around the mosque and its minaret, with the clerics and religious authorities living nearby. The bazaar, because of its position on the outskirts in relation to the old city, is open to all valley residents and outside traders. Rectangular and lined with boutiques in arcades, this is the most lively section of the city, where all sorts of products are found, from local artisanal production to the most diverse European imports. The bazaar is also the stage for specific markets: auctions, meat, and vegetable markets. The adjacent streets of the market shelter traditional professions grouped into sectors: a street of embroiderers, one for tailors, etc. However, in 1984, off-the-rack dresses were already starting to appear in the shop windows, in pastel tones, most of which came from boulevard Barbès in Paris.

1

2

OPPOSITE 1/2

A few miles away from Ghardaïa, the ksar of Beni-Isguen is the second city of M'zab. Seen from above, this neighborhood exhibits the colors that make up this modular habitat's general palette. The prevailing sand tones are accompanied by strokes of white, blue, and green, in light hues.

1

Below the rampart-houses enclosing the small city of El Atteuf, the Sidi Brahim mosque, built within a cemetery, is an important place of pilgrimage. Its architectural language brings to mind Ronchamp Chapel. In an environment governed by sand tones, three small buildings stand out against this monochromatic backdrop, each one asserting its own color identity.

2

Just off the open-market square in Ghardaïa, the small, adjacent streets are the site of smaller meat and vegetable markets, as is the case here with the El Khadra souk. From a pedestrian perspective, the pastel colors have an intensity that is reinforced by long shadows that emphasize substance and texture.

1

OPPOSITE 1 / 2 / 3 / 4 / 5
*In the narrow, winding, concentric
streets, light and color are multiplied,
highlighting the rare architectural
details of Mozabite towns, whose
architecture is a model of sobriety,
even austerity.*

1

2

3

4

5

1

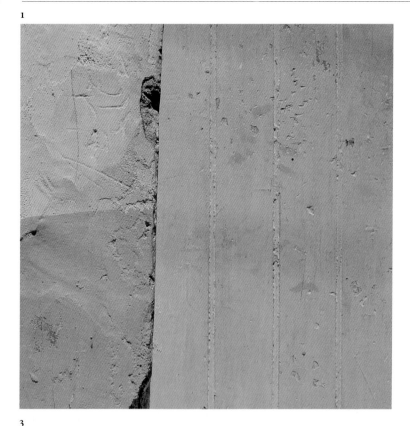

2

3

4

1 / 2 / 3 / 4

OPPOSITE 1

Strolling attentively through the small streets of M'zab cities can be enchanting and, despite the extreme sobriety of architectural language, you can observe, detail by detail, color and material compositions that take on unique pictorial qualities under the intense sunlight: a material's makeup, placement, and color assume a strongly plastic and pictorial abstract character.

1

Rigorous, coherent, simple, efficient, shunning design, expressing poverty, etc.—these words characterize the traditional architecture of M'zab cities and the practice observed by Ibadites for nine centuries. "The remarkable uniformity of M'zab, its harmony, are not the result of chance. Reason, rigor, and essence have become the focus of a choice, in an era when people were already trying to obtain technical expertise (the Ibadites were perfectly well aware of this). And out of the desired austerity, beauty emerges. The paradox is only too apparent. Mozabite rigor is not exercised randomly in appearance or line, but is applied when deeply necessary and is based on an intellectual decision about dimensions, spaces, details and the concept as a whole," writes André Ravéreau in *Le M'zab: une leçon d'architecture.*[1]

In fact, as we have seen, cities are built onto rocky peaks for reasons of defense and in order not to encroach on harvestable lands. Erecting the mosque and city enclosures are the first steps in establishing the city, then construction of the

tightly assembled homes within the ramparts had to follow a certain number of rules: orienting the house to the south, ensuring it did not cast shadow on the neighbor's property, and not showing any difference in wealth. The narrow, little streets, partly covered and often tortuous, are just large enough for two pack-mules to pass each other.

The houses, all resembling each other externally in their extreme simplicity, are built with relatively thick pebble walls, held together with plaster or *timchent*, a mortar made from Chebka gypsum. Windows are narrow slits protecting against the sun and imprudent glances. The entryway, tall and wide, is made of palm tree planks assembled with wrought-iron nails.

In the preface to Manuelle Roche's book on Ibadite architecture, Mouloud Mammeri writes that "after defining one's relationship to others, to one's brothers and to God, an individual needs to find himself in his own solace. To this end, he has built closed dwellings with a blinding wall that shields

against outside noises, services, and conventions. Even once inside the door, the vestibule is furnished with a final partition creating a blind entryway."[2]

Today these houses, which were formerly left the natural color of the material or whitewashed in lime, radiate the luminous tones of their coatings in every shade of pink and yellow ochre, relatively robust blues, with a few facades done in green and mauve.

1. André Ravéreau, *Le M'zab: une leçon d'architecture.* Paris: Sindbad, 1987.
2. Manuelle Roche, *Le M'zab: architecture Ibadite en Algérie.* Paris: Arthaud, 1970.

1

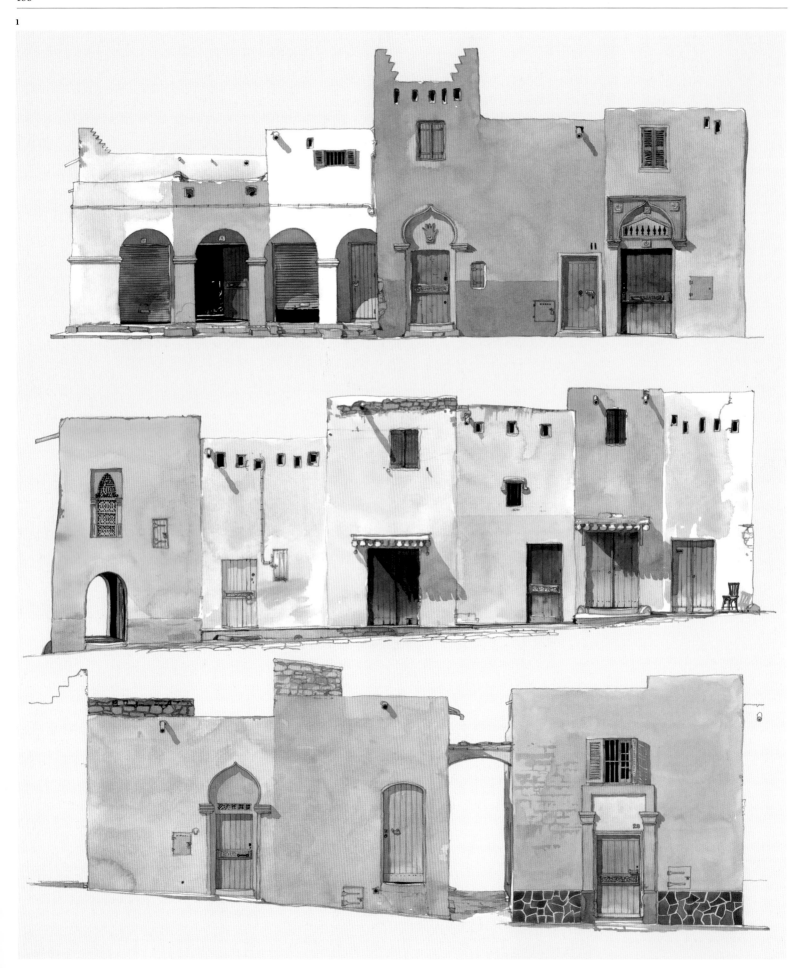

1

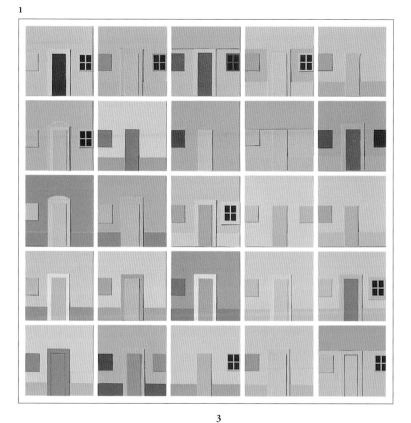

2

3

4

5

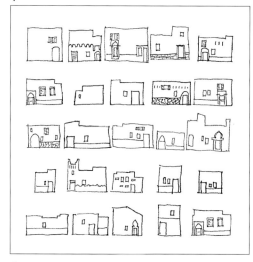

6

1/2
These two charts, showing chromatic notations made along the narrow streets of Ghardaïa in 1984, illustrate two important details: first, facade colors are largely governed by sand tones; second, blue and pink are well represented on external walls, but green does not come into play here because it is mainly used for interior patios and terraces. The tones of the selective palette normally belong to the same register as those of the general palette, but are used to form contrasting zones of hot and cold.

3/5/6
A few combinations with pink from facades in Ghardaïa. Seeing these tonalities reminds us that, in architecture, color and substance become one.

4
Small sketches of catalogued homes that comprise the synthesizing chart.

OPPOSITE 1
This watercolor illustrates on a few facades the colors used for homes in M'zab, which cluster around sand and ochre tones: blue, turquoise, pink, and green animate the urban environment, either on the general or selective palette.

Morocco

Ouarzazate and Southern Morocco

Ouarzazate, located between the High- (Haut) Atlas and the Anti-Atlas Mountains, is the doorway to the pre-Saharan desert. This city is at the crossroads of the Dra Valley and Dades Valley, which are lined with verdant oases and earthen villages that form exceptional architectural structures against the desert landscape.

The Dra River spills forth from where the Dades River intersects the Ouarzazate River, each originating in the High Atlas. It starts by carving a ragged path between the mountainous folds of the Saghro and Sioura ranges, over a distance of about 37 miles (60 kilometers); the canyon is impressive with its black rocks and complete lack of vegetation and animal life.

1

1
The old village of Tabuki, planted along the Dra river, displays earthen shapes that are in color harmony with the vast desert landscape surrounding it.

In the foreground, along the riverbeds, white salt stands in contrast, creating a brightness scale for the various ochre tones of the sand and soil.

After the small city of Agdz is, surprisingly, an oasis: palm, orange, lemon, almond, and olive trees are surrounded by patches of fertile ground lavishly producing grains and feed. And from there, all along the Dra, from Agdz to Mhamid, is a succession of six long palm groves, each growing the three types of vegetation that are common to Saharan oases: palm trees, fruit trees, and grains. The country's wealth comes from water, a resource utilized to its maximum benefit with the help of irrigation canals. There is something magical about seeing this clear water flowing through the desert.

Here in this landscape of contrasts, where cultivated zones live among desert spaces, stand impressive stone villages, or *ksour*, generally on rocky peaks, sometimes forming relatively important districts, and formerly protected by the city walls against attacks by nomads who were drawn to the fertile valley. The red-ochre adobe walls, penetrated by a single doorway, are decorated with balustrades and arcades and flanked by crenellated towers. Within the ksar, streets form an even network, with a long axial artery almost always facing southeast and cut into secondary streets at right angles. A collective granary (agadir) allows each family to store grain in its own space. The houses are composed of squared rooms, a traditional patio, and a sort of dark well that guarantees maximum coolness when the outside heat becomes intense, as it often does in the valley.

1

1
Nineteen miles (30 kilometers) from Zagora, the road borders the imposing village of Assurer, which stretches horizontally along palm groves.

The architectural language's overall sobriety is moderated with refined angles and stair patterns. Openings add their invaluable punctuation to the general rhythm of this mineral landscape (Dra Valley).

1

1

Along the Asif Mellah, a river secluded in verdant gardens, the old village of Aït Ben Haddou acts as a historic testament to traditional kasbah architecture. The layering of simple adobe cubes becomes a rhythmic script in a play of light and shadow. This village was the site of a meticulous restoration project.

2

2

With towers for defense, the kasbah of Caïd Tamrougad stands in a strategic position between the Dra oasis and the barrier wall of Atlas Mountains. This landscape's permanent colors are governed by the warm earthen brown and purplish brown of the mountain slopes. The impermanent colors come from the blue of the sky, the greens of the vegetation, and the changing reflections in the waters of the Dra.

The houses here are made with local soil: slightly moistened by the workers, it is poured into a framework of planks and compacted with a wood pestle by the head mason, the *maalen*. The roof terrace is made with a bed of branches covered in soil at a slight incline in order facilitate rain drainage.

Adobe is a fragile material and, if it is not protected against the elements, can return to the soil from which it came. Architects now know the means necessary to preserve this exceptional heritage: constructing a stone wall on the most exposed side, coating the exteriors, and insulating ground walls with bituminous felt. Still today, builders use the same construction materials, according to the same

principles and order, but a few inhabitants are leaving the ksour to look elsewhere in Morocco for less limited economic activity. In fact, Dra's population, comprising Arabs and Berbers, often mixed with darker-skinned Haratines, is dedicated essentially to artisanry: weaving, leatherwork, and pottery.

1

The Dades Valley is worthy of its nickname, the "valley of a thousand kasbahs." The kasbah in Souk el Khemir, with its earthen colors, exhibits elegant proportions and a decorative refinement along the tops of the walls, which are made of raw brick decorated with recessed nooks and relief.

2

This very sober facade exposes its wall patches by the presence of soil that is slightly different in color than the soil on site, creating a sort of monochromatic composition. The deep blue door stands out strongly against the overall mineral backdrop of earth and stone (Imassine, in the Dra Valley).

3

Protected by high brick walls, these two kasbahs, which are nearly identical and relatively recent, stand on the desert plain that stretches to the Dades Valley. Ground and architecture meld in perfect chromatic harmony. In the distance, beyond the valley, stand the high Atlas barriers.

Still within the Dra Valley there is another example of earthen architecture: the *kasbah*, a sort of castle occupying a strategic location and resembling the castle strongholds of Europe with four corner towers. Kasbahs in this region are very reminiscent of Aït ben Haddou's kasbah, built on a hill not far from Ouarzazate on the road to Marrakech. This grouping, a pure example of Berber architecture with its high enclosures watched over by towers with small openings meant for surveillance and defense, displays a unique architectural character with its decorated kasbahs and numerous homes all built on the same model. One single color dominates: the red of the exterior walls rising out of mounds of the same color. This ensemble is in the midst of restoration and for the time being, residents are housed in temporary dwellings, waiting to return to their homes which are being restored to their original state with local material and according to traditional methods.

Yet it is in the Dades Valley that this type of architecture is most frequently represented, so much so that the road that crosses the oases in this valley has been nicknamed the "kasbah route." Upon leaving Ouarzazate, vast desert expanses extend along the High Atlas, whose summits remain covered with snow until June, creating a powerful contrast between the snow-capped mountains and pebbly desert so proudly traversed by a few camels. Next comes the Dades Valley, followed by the palm groves of Skoura, a large village ringed by rosebushes whose distilled flowers produce rosewater, a product widely sold in this region.

Approaching El-Kelaa-des-Mgouna is the "cold" oasis: because palm trees do not grow in higher altitudes, room has been left for cultivated gardens, poplar trees, willow and fruit trees, and everywhere, thousands of rosebushes. Next comes a rapid succession of villages all the way to Boumalne, with ochre-colored ksours and kasbahs dominating the cliffs all along the river.

Unlike the Dra Valley, the Dades Valley escaped control by nomadic populations, but came under threat of raids by neighboring tribes. This is why, in the seventeenth century, the mountain clans who established the oasis began building ksours and kasbahs, residential units capable of ensuring their protection. It is likely that certain ksours date back before 1800.

While the fortified collective hamlet—*ksar* in Arabic and *irherm* in Berber—was the first type of dwelling in Dades, family castles—*tirhermt* or *tiguemmi* in Berber—often called kasbahs—were constructed much later by families who left the hamlet, often for lack of space. These kasbahs bring together elegance and sturdiness; the thick adobe walls are raised on stone foundations and built up in the ksour framing technique. Building soil is chosen with care for its robustness, beauty, and uncommon coloring. During the drying process, the walls become quite hard, but it is crucial to protect them against weathering with a soil coating that is often mixed with broken-up straw, which is resistant to rain. Older kasbahs have up to six or seven floors, of which only the upper sections are decorated with the help of coated, raw bricks that form bands and geometric friezes; the decorative bricks may also be laid at an angle, a technique that is not found in the Dra Valley. Following an ancient architectural process, tall corner towers whose walls are always angled and are slightly curved, flank these small castles.

1

1 / 2 / 3 / 4

OPPOSITE 1

Climbing through the streets of the old neighborhoods in and around Ouarzazate, it is interesting to discover how the metalwork doors are decorated. The elongated diamond form is a frequently used figure: is it an allusion to the symbolic meeting of earth and sky?

The color on the sheet metal pannel is Van Dyck brown. In figure 1, you can distinguish the parallel between tradition and modernity with the juxtaposition of wood and metal doors.

1/2/3/4/5/6/7/8/9
Doors and gates show off the resident's desire to personalize his home by decorating the entryways with form and color. Careful attention is given to masonry framework, which is often decorated with ceramic tiles or encrusted mosaics. On metal doors, *geometric and floral patterns brighten the otherwise austere architectural ensemble (Ouarzazate).*

1

1
*With contrasting colors and materials,
there is a peculiar confrontation
between the dried earth of the
masonry and the polished stainless
steel of the door, a warped and
immobile mirror reflecting the earth
and sky (El-Kelaa-des-Mgouna).*

1

2

We have noticed that traditional large homes are currently being replaced by large, yet lower, buildings that, with their angled towers, replicate the kasbah in a simplified form. The homes of El Kelaa-des-Mgouna and its surrounding areas are made of light ochre adobe with infrequent, small doors protected by a sculpted, wrought-iron gate painted in blue, green, ochre, or brown. We could be concerned, like D. Jacques-Meunié who, in his well-documented text on Dades habitats, wrote, "Since 1940, as a result of the World War, traditions are disappearing and the architectural art of Dades is in complete disrepair. The purity of line and the finesse of proportions is no longer found in more recent constructions, which are for the most part short and cubic, with exteriors striped with chiseling."[1] Or, we could be enthusiastic like Jean Dethier, for whom "it is almost a miracle of history that rural and urban populations knew how to diligently preserve, from one generation to the next, this admirable thousand-year-old tradition, while endlessly adapting it to new needs so that it has survived—intact—until today."[2]

In Ouarzazate, the administrative capital of Dra, the imposing Taourirt kasbah is striking for its enormous mass and smooth, earthen murals that hang over the oued. It's a veritable conglomeration formed by a series of kasbahs that are fit together and drawn into a narrow enclosure for the purpose of defense. In this architecture, elements of detail are abundant and certain towers are decorated with very elaborate, hollowed-out motifs. This relatively recent kasbah is inhabited by a large and rather poor population, and the narrow streets are filled with children who attempt to win several dirhams by improvising for guides and their kindly tourists.

1. D. Jacques-Meunié, *Architectures et habitats du Dadès*. Paris: Librairie C. Klincksieck, 1962.
2. Jean Dethier, *Architectures de terre, ou l'avenir d'une tradition millénaire*. Paris: Editions du Centre Pompidou, 1986.

1

1/2

OPPOSITE 1/2
Whether public or private, Moroccan architecture today shows the lasting imprint of traditional Berber culture. These recent constructions in Ouarzazate have matching general palettes of earthen gray and ochre, strongly accented by the selective palette of the white frames, that decorate the facades and run along the architectural molding. The metal doors, fashioned by hand, are patterned and decorated with various designs.

2

1

2

3

1 / 2 / 3
*In southern Morocco, windows are
never very large, in order to keep the
heat out. Sculpted grills, reminiscent of
mousharabiehs, protect painted
carpentry (Ouarzazate).*

Also in Ouarzazate, but this time in the outlying neighborhoods where there is already a bit of desert with pebbly soil where rocks flourish and vegetation does not, the current modern architecture caught our attention and was the focus of a specific site study. The new houses are made of cinder blocks and covered in a greenish-gray or brownish-gray cement coating, in a tone colder than adobe; they are taller than traditional earthen homes and the apertures are larger. On the ground floor, colonnades hang over a covered gallery intended for commerce.

In March 1995, the city of Elkouds, an extension of Ouarzazate located between the city center and the airport, was still a large construction site where a few apartment buildings and one- to two-story townhouses were in the midst of construction. These boxes exhibit facades with jutting volumes of balconies and loggias. Despite an apparent repetitiveness, none of these homes with roof terraces resembles its neighbor; the narrow openings are decorated with grates and patterns that make them unique and the sheet-metal doors are fashioned by hand and worked into various decorative patterns. As for the general palette, it is dominated by earthen tonalities of gray-amber stucco, tinted with warm as well as colder tones. The selective palette is characterized above all by netting and delicate geometric patterns that decorate the facade and work off the molding; the metallic doors, window gratings, and balconies are usually brown in tone.

1

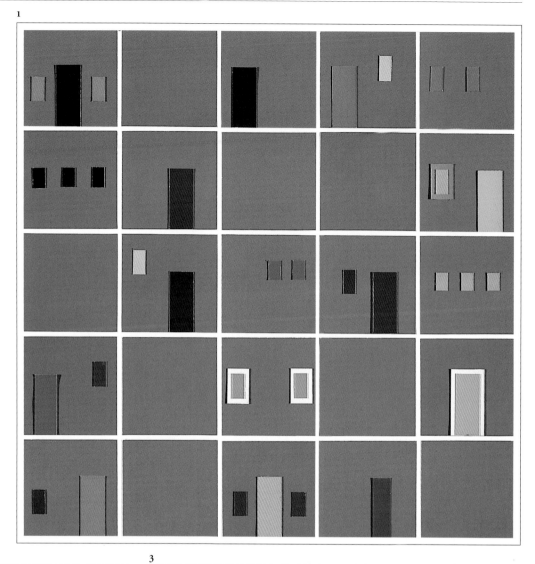

1
This chart assembles the chromatic data from twenty-five houses in the Tifoultout kasbah in the Dra Valley, expressing the general palette of earthen browns. In terms of selective palette tones, either they form a simple contrast of browns with the general palette, or they contrast more strongly with blue and green tones.

2/3
Within the decorative repertory of Berber architecture, terraces are often enhanced with graded merlons that create a rhythm along the principal horizontal lines. The textured wall treatment lends character to the ochre tones of the cob facades.

The selective colors of the iron-clad windows are in blue and green tones here, offering a cool contrast to the warmer general palette (Dades Valley).

1

1

2

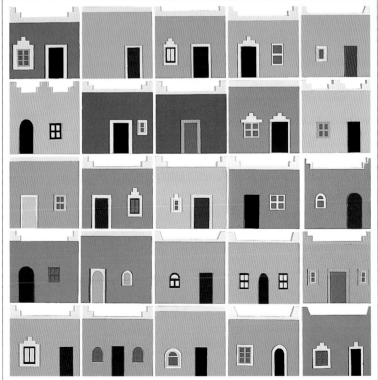

1

This private home in the city of Elkouds, an extension of Ouarzazate, is characterized by the clean lines of its architectural language and the Mars-violet color of its coating.

2

The twenty-five house models assembled on this chart summarize the dominant colors in the new city of Elkouds, studied in March 1995. These cinder block residences are covered in coats of refined and delicate hues. The soils and sands balance out grays that range from neutral to warm and cold. The selective palette is strongly marked by the nearly ubiquitous presence of white, used in framing lines, ironwork, and steplike merlons. The metal doors are generally brown in tone.

OPPOSITE 1

South Moroccan residences, both traditional and modern, are characterized by a range of earthen colors: from the multilevel kasbah to recent, suburban homes around Ouarzazate, browns, pink ochre, and red ochre make up the general palette. On urban dwellings, the Berber-inspired designs are trimmed in white.

IRAN

YAZD

The city of Yazd is located in the heart of Iran, an immense country, two thirds of which is desert. It is as large as France, Great Britain, Italy, and Spain combined. All around, the desert sands sweep over the city whenever there is a wind. This desert was the motivation for building Yazd, during an era when camel caravans crossed from oasis to oasis. As with Ghardaia in southern Algeria, Yazd is a symbol of the determination of people who decided to settle in an arid natural setting. The residents' survival was only possible because of a network of ghanats, underground canals that carry water to the city from Chirkouh, a mountain range that reaches 13,123 feet (4,000 meters) in altitude. Today, drinking water is provided to each home by a well in the courtyard, while ghanat water is merely used for troughs and for irrigating palm groves and orchards.

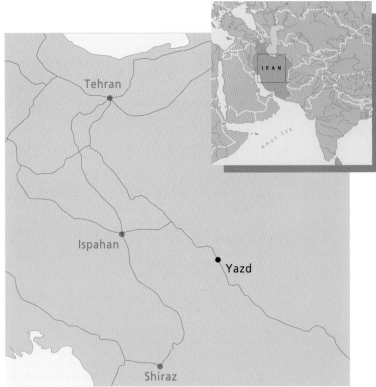

1

2

1/2
A traditional desert city, Yazd stretches to the horizon with its pisé, or raw brick, constructions of earth and sand colors. These photos, taken at different moments of the day, demonstrate how the same material can vary in tone with the change in daylight.

On the dome of the Seyyed Rokneddin mausoleum, dedicated to a saint who lived in the fourteenth century and built of hand-cut ceramic, turquoise blue dominates as a symbol of the sky. Along the base of the dome, two strips of ikufi calligraphy spell out quotations from the Koran.

1

1
Every house has a badguir—*a
ventilation system, in use since the
Middle Ages, that carries the cooling
wind across rooms and out over the
water of the interior gardens.*

At the beginning of the first millennium, during the Sassanid era, Yazd (or Yezd) was an important Zoroastrian center. The city, taken by Arabs in the seventh century, was saved in 1220 by Mongol hordes. In the fourteenth century, the Mozaffarids built splendid mosques: the Friday Mosque and the Institute of Time and the Hour, as well as even more ancient monuments such as the Mausoleum for Twelve Imams that dates to the eleventh century.

Since the Muslim conquest, Yazd has been, along with Kerman, a refuge for Zoroastrian communities. Their religious practices are hardly different from those of the Parsis, their exiled brethren in India, who have remained faithful to the ancient Persian religion preached by Zoroaster in the sixth century B.C.; they believe in a supreme being whom they honor by leading respectable lives and performing a few rites: maintaining the holy fire that, in their eyes, is the image of divinity; performing an initiation ceremony around the time of adolescence, as well as a very particular funeral ceremony; and, in order not to desecrate the land and water, leaving bodies of the dead for the vultures on the interior stairs of a concealing tower, known as the Tower of Silence, located several miles from the city. The Guebres, or Zoroastrians, were for a long time the victims of Muslim bullying, the latter considering them to be infidels: men were forced to wear a special turban and gaudy shoes that made them easy to identify, and they were not allowed to carry umbrellas, wear glasses, or wear the colors blue, black, green, or bright red. They lived with their families in a special neighborhood and certain professions were forbidden them. During our study, these forms of discrimination no longer existed and the communities had begun to integrate.

For centuries, the economy in Yazd has been based mainly on textiles. Long ago, Yazd almost had a monopoly on silk mills, and it is no surprise that it garnered the admiration of Marco Polo, who saw in it "a very good and noble trading city. Many splendid fabrics of gold and silk, called "yazdis," are manufactured there." The quality of its artisanry helped spare the city from the Mongols and Timurids, and led it to be commissioned by the Great Mongols of India to produce their ceremonial dress. In the nineteenth century, nine thousand artisans worked with silk in eighteen hundred workshops, but poppy was partially replacing blackberries in the fields, until the government prohibited the production of opium. It was in this way that the development of rug artisans and the semi-artisanal weaving of fabrics—cotton and synthetic—occurred.

The geographic factors—building the city in a desert region—as well as climatic factors—hot, dry summers, long, cold winters, and sandstorms—have strongly contributed to the elaboration of a unique architecture, adapted to the site's limitations. Yazd is a traditional city, whose essential quality is that it is mainly composed of adobe houses behind courts and gardens, concealed from sight by thick, monochromatic adobe walls. In 1966, more than 85 percent of homes were in adobe and raw clay brick, dating from the nineteenth century and the beginning of the twentieth century. The most dilapidated houses have been replaced by baked-brick or stone constructions, which also punctuate the main arteries of the newer residential neighborhoods, while traditional adobe has been abandoned in favor of materials that are more modern and solid.

1
Samples taken from Yazd in 1976 are authentic records of the construction materials used. The mixed fragments of architectural and domestic ceramics evoke a selective palette dominated by blue tones.

1

Taken overlooking the Djame mosque, this photo reveals the overlapping, earthen domes and terraces that are characteristic of Yazd rooftops.

A few trees emerge from the patios, evoking the intimacy of interior gardens. In this district of dye artisans, freshly dyed wools add their bright, random colors to the mineral landscape.

1

Our study concerns the ancient part of the city, crisscrossed by narrow roads surrounded by high adobe walls that offer sun protection and are often topped with ribbed vaulting in raw brick covered with pisé. These blind walls hide social stature and the lifestyle of the traditional homes' inhabitants. The bazaars—the principal axes of commercial activity—are topped by small adobe cupolas so close to one another that they form a single roof. Light penetrates through a small, circular opening in the center of each. Everywhere, the construction material used is earth, in the form of adobe for walls that surround houses and gardens, and in the form of sun-dried brick for walls and roofs of the more traditional homes, which are subsequently covered with cob, a relatively solid coating since it only needs to be refreshed once every ten or fifteen years.

The use of brick, first dried in the sun then cooked in an oven, is a very old method, originating most likely in prehistoric Iran. This material offers considerable advantages: in its standard format, brick is light, resistant, and its suppleness makes it earthquake-resistant; furthermore, brick is an excellent thermal insulator. For the construction of houses, Me'Mar—the traditional architect—and his masons are solicited, and workers are recruited for the day;[1] they dig up the earth on the land itself in order to fabricate the bricks. What follows is a chromatic rapport between habit and environment so closely knit—even organic in nature—that you can truly speak of homochromy.

1. The thesis of Sima Hafezi-Kouban on Yazd testifies to a profound study on the diverse aspects of life in this part of the Iranian desert. Sima-Hafezi Kouban, *Yazd: Face à la "modernization,"* (third year thesis, Sociology, Paris VII, 1975).

1

The badguir that stands atop each residence provides ventilation. This construction shows all types of labor techniques for working with clay, both dried and baked.

2

Along the ancient ramparts, the dominant earth—ground and walls— gives this area a monochromatic character, enhanced here by the impermanent foliage of vegetation.

Here, the color of the habitat is closely linked to rhythms and proportions, which are imposed for the most part by the material being used, the method of construction, and the climatic constraints. The use of cupolas is in response to technical and climatic imperatives: with sunrays only hitting a portion of the cupola, the shaded portion helps maintain a cooler temperature inside; in addition, the constantly blowing winds help lower the temperature. In public buildings, double cupolas—even more efficient—are common.

The badguir, still widely in use despite its age, is a way to aerate the home. It consists of a sort of chimney, most often four-sided, which draws in the wind and initiates an air current that keeps fresh air circulating through the room.

Zoroastrian homes were not allowed to have these ventilating towers for air circulation, because Muslims were supposed to be able to reach the edge of their roofs. Thus, Zoroastrians dug out their floors in order to create a more livable space. In addition, their homes were outlined in white plaster to make them more easily identifiable.

The only spots of color that interrupt the monochrome wash of the city come from the mosques, of which there are more than fifty in Yazd. The cupola of the Djame, or Friday mosque is covered in enameled bricks dominated by turquoise blue, which is symbolic of the sky. The geometric patterns decorating Islamic monuments create an intricate mosaic that shimmers in the sun like a veritable jewel.

1

1
This view overlooking an interior courtyard of the Djame mosque shows off the light colors of baked bricks. Beyond the desert, in the distance, stand the profiles of the surrounding mountains.

The colors of the habitat's selective palette are limited to the colors painted onto wooden doors, which are usually recessed double-doors facing the street; they are constructed of wide, vertical planks of wood with two crossbars mounted with wrought-iron nails. Windows, on the other hand, are not visible to passers-by, being concealed by the exterior wall.

Plant life, an impermanent element, adds the freshness of its shade and tonalities: the most popular tree is the pomegranate, as it seldom needs to be watered. A wide variety of fruit trees and plants around the fountain of interior courtyards offer their shade and mellow the intensity of heat and light. Reflecting the sky above, fountains, with their spray of water as a figure of perpetual movement, do not only have a symbolic function: they are used for domestic work and provide a source of coolness.

Around the time of our study, in 1975, Yazd was exhibiting an exceptionally coherent urban fabric in its makeup. Architectural uniformity, reinforced by an extremely sober general palette, was taking on a very distinct character under the captivating desert light. In fact, the pureness of the air and the intensity of sunlight reflection help to transform the color effects of the pigmentation, giving the architecture extraordinary highlights.

1

3

2

1
This assemblage of dried fruits and beans shows a splendid range of natural hues in every shade.

2
The entry gate to a private garden near the city. The wood door, the dried clay bricks, and adobe form a monochrome of natural tones accented by contrasting materials.

3
Material samples—soil, brick, plaster—are of great importance during the review of chromatic data obtained from a site.

1 / 2
The woodwork along streets and courtyards offers the only spots of color and contrast with the neutral tones of the masonry.

3
The courtyard of the Djame mosque with brick flooring laid out in decorative, right-angled patterns.

4
The door of an older residence, with interior horizontal supports held on by wrought-iron nails. The contrasting colors of the young girl's clothing harmonize with the bluish-green of the door.

1/2
Persia played a major role in the development of ceramic tilework, first in the East and then in the West, particularly in Spain and Portugal.

These hand-cut mosaics form a sacred language in honor of Ali (1) and Allah (2).

1

2

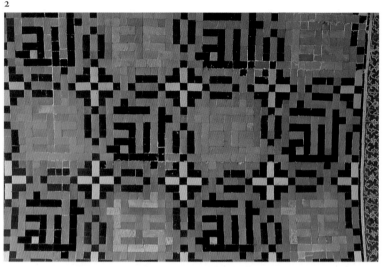

3

4

3/4
These verses from the Koran are traced in white against a blue background in the Tuluth style dominated by curved lines.

1
*A detail of floral decorations on
ceramic tiles.*

1
This old, studded door, covered in a lapis-lazuli lacquer, stands out against the light brick masonry arranged in geometric patterns.

1

2

1 / 2
Whether painted or in natural woods, these old, studded doors are a testament to ancestral know-how.

3
Ceramic fragments and plaster samples in a range of tones that include a variety of blues.

3

1

2

3

4

1 / 2 / 3 / 4
Since antiquity, brick has been a modular material that, beyond its functional qualities, allows for a wide range of compositions. The diversity of tone comes from the makeup of the soils used and from the baking method.

In Yazd, despite their various pigmentations, bricks are generally situated in a range of light and dark yellow ochres.

1

2

3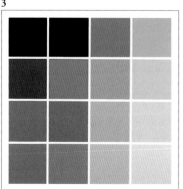

4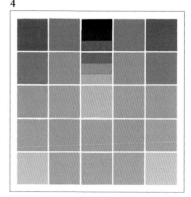

5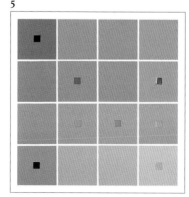

1
In the Iranian desert, city habitats are limited to the colors of local sands and soils, producing a remarkably unified, homochromatic effect.

The only colored elements visible to passers-by are doors and gates that open onto the street; they are left natural or painted in green, blue, and turquoise tones.

2
Yazd's general palette is centered in a range of earthy yellow-ochre tones, from the palest to the deepest (site study completed in 1975).

3
The selective palette of Yazd's architecture is dominated by a range of blues and turquoise-blues.

4/5
These two charts illustrate the punctuating blues of detail elements and their contrast with earthen ochre tones of the predominant architectural surfaces.

YEMEN

The two regions that we studied in April 1996 once again belong to the Republic of Yemen; both had been split into the Arab Republic of Yemen (northern Yemen) and the People's Democratic Republic of Yemen (southern Yemen) in the nineteenth century after the British settled into Aden in 1839. The current Republic of Yemen, established on May 22, 1990 following a very rapid reunification process, has recovered its cultural, historic, and geographic unity.

Named the root *ymn*, Yemen is a country of happiness and rectitude—"Arabia felix" as it was known in ancient times—which offers its residents the fruits of a fertile land, thanks to its climate. Its topography is split into five very distinct regions: the Zaydite area, a mountainous region that is home to most of the large cities of northern Yemen, notably the capital city Sana'a; an agriculturally rich central region, whose capital is Taiz; Tihama with its hot, humid climate, along the Red sea; the south Yemeni coastline encompassing the city of Aden; and finally, Jawl, and the valley of Hadramaout.

Our color study was carried out in two of these regions, each one quite different from the other: on one hand was Sana'a with its surrounding lands of northern Yemen, and on the other was the oasis of Hadramaout and its three main cities—Seyun, Tarim, and Shibam—in southern Yemen. On northern Yemen's high plateaus, whose summits reach heights of 11,483 feet (3,500 meters), the essentially rural population farms on small plots of terraced land with the help of constant labor and a temperate climate, supplying the majority of the country's agricultural produce: fruits, vegetables, grains (sorghum, barley, wheat, and corn—the

staples of Yemeni cooking), and coffee, whose production continues to diminish as khat—the only farm product that is on the rise today—continues to monopolize the better lands. Khat is a part of popular tradition: after lunch, men buy their ration of freshly cut soft, green leaves that they chew slowly, all the while smoking many cigarettes and drinking Pepsi. All activity slows to the point of stopping, until evening. With food production waning and the population on the rise, Yemen is nowadays forced to import large quantities of grain.

1

1

OPPOSITE 1

These two pages highlight Yemen's geographic and architectural diversity—the North, left, and the South, right—reunified in 1990. The landscape on the left plunges us into secular Yemen where walled villages stand on rocky peaks of the high plateaus that have been terraced to grow vegetables, grains, coffee, and khat. The village of Banu Mora, on the eastern slope of Djebel Haraz, is a perfect example of the monochromy that exists between sandstone buildings and their mineral surroundings. Like a mirage, Shibam stands in the immense desert of Hadramaout, in southern Yemen. The plaster coating applied to certain sections of buildings strongly reflects the sunlight and reinforces the unusual character of this monumental, earthen architecture, whose modernity is surprising.

1

1

Looking over the old neighborhoods of Sana'a, the "city with six hundred minarets," you discover the incomparable architecture and decorative theatricality of Yemen's capital city, built 7,546 feet (2,300 meters) high in a ring of mountains.

The cityscape's chromatic uniformity comes from the details of its elements with, on the one hand, a general palette dominated gray-ochre clay bricks and, on the other, a selective palette consisting of decorative patterns trimmed in white lime.

The demographic explosion taking place in this country is due in part to a high birthrate (it is not uncommon to see families with 10 or more children), and also to the return in 1990 of a million Yemeni people who had been forced to leave Saudi Arabia. The social fabric is quite complex and rests on a hierarchical system based on profession, religion, and whether one lives in the country or city. We happened to be in Sana'a during the Aïd religious festival which commemorates Abraham's sacrifice. Several days before the celebration, and especially the evening before the big feast, the city was already bustling with excitement: whole families poured into the *souk*, or open squares, in search of new clothing (white and blue Saudi-style *djellabas*, vests sold by screaming merchants), children grouped in the middle of the street painted the faded jambiyas[1] in a light, emerald green, and sheep waited patiently to be sold for family dinners. Along with the jambiya, which is both a weapon and adornment, men's dress is traditionally composed of a shirt and skirt, the *futa*; turbans are *de rigueur*, and a shawl worn over the shoulders distinguishes newlywed men. Women go in public dressed completely, their faces entirely veiled in black, draped in long Indian fabrics with patterns in red and blue, known as *sitara*. In Sana'a, not even their eyes are visible, and their hands are often gloved in black.

The region's staple food is the sorghum pancake, which is baked in a round oven and served with vegetables and fenugreek, a grain reputed to have energizing and curative properties.

1. A jambiya is a knife with a curved blade worn by men and adolescent boys.

1 / 2
One of the particularities of the urban layout of Sana'a comes from the presence, here and there, of vegetable gardens right in the heart of the old city. These small islands of vegetation lend a peaceful and refreshing air to an urban landscape that is otherwise quite mineral.

The residents in neighboring homes come to work here in the coolness of evening, before nightfall.

1

Yemenis, whether northern or southern, are master engineers. The homes that they build by hand blend perfectly into the landscape, to the point of merging with it. The traditional principles that govern how each habitat is to be conceived, whether in stone, brick, or clay, came from the need for protection against outside aggressors, on the one hand, and the need to maximize harvestable lands on the other. Therefore, there are few scattered homes; instead, villages and towns stand strong against their enemies with the high, impenetrable walls of family apartment buildings forming a solid, windowless rampart.

1/2

Upon black basalt foundations rise one or two stories of limestone, with brick appearing above. Decorative bands and geometric friezes of cut brick, slightly in relief, outline each floor and frame each window. The architectural molding is also outlined in a thick plaster wash. During the 1980s, UNESCO signed on to save the old neighborhood of Sana'a and to renovate its tower-houses.

2

1

1
This group of residences bordering vegetable gardens is a good example of the chromatic identity of older apartment houses in Sana'a. The general palette takes its color from basalt, soil, brick, and plaster; the selective palette consists of the tones from design elements and carpentry, with the expressive force of the blue doors along the ground floor.

Those are the permanent colors. The impermanent colors are the green of the plant life and the blue of the sky; vehicles, especially the bright yellow mail truck, add random colors.

1

2

3

4

1

2

3

4

1 / 2 / 3 / 4
OPPOSITE 1 / 2 / 3 / 4
Metal doors and gates are fashioned by metalsmiths who reinforce them with horizontal and vertical strips and then solder on creative shapes in inventive ways (Sana'a and its surroundings).

The patterns that they form are highlighted with forcefully contrasting colors (Sana'a and environs).

The layout of Yemeni cities, which were not the result of urban planning, is characteristic of Islamic tradition, except that residences open onto the street, whereas Arab homes are usually built around an interior courtyard onto which all the windows open. The living room, or *mafrij*, built on the upper floor of the home, offers a panoramic view of the surrounding countryside. Yemeni taste in exterior design is also contrary to Saudi Arabian standards. Its architectural character is thought to date back to pre-Islamic cultures, influenced perhaps by Mesopotamia.

NORTH YEMEN

Northern Yemeni architecture is all the more surprising for visitors because it was left unknown for so long, Yemen remaining the second most closed society, after Tibet, until 1962. Sana'a, the capital, located in a ring of mountains 7,546 feet (2,300 meters) high, has been well known for almost 2,000 years, and is believed to have been founded by Shem, the son of Noah.

The old, walled city is a veritable architectural gem, a treasure of world cultural history preserved through UNESCO. Sana'a is made up of three urban centers: the old Arab city, dominated by a citadel with a central souk that is one of the oldest on the Arabian peninsula, and, here and there, vegetable gardens that provide revenue for the neighboring mosque; the Jewish quarter, where houses were limited to two floors and all exterior decoration was prohibited; and the Turkish quarter, whose houses, built in the sixteenth century, are surrounded by extensive gardens.

1

2

3

1/2/3
OPPOSITE 1/2/3
Whether in the city or country, traditional architecture in northern Yemen is enchanting in the diversity and richness of its structural and formal elements, augmented by countless friezes and patterns that highlight the molding. The windows of the upper floors are often crowned with an arched stained-glass window in geometric and floral patterns that light up at nightfall in bright and contrasting colors (1 Kahil; 2 Manakha; 3 Wadi Dhar; opposite, 1 / 3 Manakha; 2 Kawkaban).

1

The architecture in old Sana'a is characterized by tower-topped homes, six or seven stories high, a style that became popular several centuries before Christ. The ground floor and second floor are destined for animals and food supplies, the third floor for servants, the next three floors for women and children, and the top floor for the head of the household, with a large receiving room that opens up to the outside. The color palette for traditional homes comes from the different building materials that are used: on black basalt foundations, a floor or two rise up in ochre limestone patterned with horizontal stripes and designs in black lava-stone. Pink sandstone and green basalt alternate in arches and lintels. The polychromatic effect of the stone illustrates a very old, southern Arabian tradition, which in Sana'a, is visible on the Al-Qalis cathedral and the Palace of Ghamdan. Brick, a lighter, less expensive, solid material, appears above a few stone levels.

The master mason displays all of his skill and creativity in the decorative bands that are designed at the same time the walls are built: he shapes the bricks into triangles or diamonds; the bricks, jutting slightly from the wall, are coated in plaster and enliven the exterior with their layout, color, and composition. The patterns are emphasized by the shifting light, giving the architecture in Sana'a an enchanted feel that resonates at night in a burst of brightly colored stained glass—yellow, red, green, and blue—hanging in windows.

What is fascinating in Sana'a and what sets it apart is that all of these admirably built and decorated homes exhibit an overall architectural and chromatic unity in spite of their diversity.

Trade expansion and the arrival of new materials on the market, concrete and its conglomerates on the one hand, prefabricated carpentry and metallic doors on the other, which are less expensive than wood, brick, and stone, point to a profound move away from the ancestral conception of the building arts. In their remarkable work, Pascal Maréchaux and Paul Bonnenfant are investigating the old city's preservation and the state of its future.[1]

2

3

1. *Sana'a: parcours d'une cité d'Arabie,* under the direction of Pascal Maréchaux. Paris: Institut du Monde Arabe, 1987; Paul Bonnenfant, *Les Maisons-tour de Sana'a.* Paris: CNRS, 1989.

1

Founded in the twelfth century, the
citadel of Al-Hajjara rises up above a
craggy cliff. The tower-houses, built
one against the other, form a veritable
rampart against invaders. This is one
of the most beautiful examples of
mountain architecture in Yemen.

2

Whether concerning the foundation
stones or the bricks of the upper floors,
building materials in this elevated city
are perfectly homochromatic with the
pink sandstone of the mountainside.
The design of each facade is generally
based on a symmetrical division of
openings that embrace creativity and
are underscored by decorative patterns
(Wadi Dhar).

Not far from Sana'a, to the east of the capital, the towns and villages of Manakha, Kahil, Shibam, Kawkaban, Thula, Amran, Al-Hajjara, etc., are home to architectural treasures. Each of these places, typical in their northern Yemeni construction, has a clean appearance expressed by the choice of materials and their layout, and in decorative effects and architectural detail.

The fortified villages, built in sandstone or basalt, cling to rocky peaks, with which they start to merge. The houses rise up high, forming ramparts, guaranteeing protection to the residents and leaving harvestable land untouched. The coloring of the stone actively participates in the specific character of each location: red sandstone in Kawkaban, yellow sandstone in Thula, a mix of different colored minerals in Manakha, stone in Al-Hajjara that darkens with oxidation, red sandstone in Al-Hutayb, and every surprising tone of basalt, from light violet to emerald green!

1

1
The old city of Manakha is a bustling commercial center that stretches along the foot of the Djebel Shibam, along the way from Sana'a to Tihama. As if projected on a wall, the cubist composition of this neighborhood takes on an unreal dimension of a theatrical backdrop. You can sense the magic power that light has over the landscape's colors and forms. Its random and ephemeral character comes through in the beauty of these fleeting moments.

1

2

3

4

1/2/3/4
All over the north, in brick, stone, and clay, architecture displays the Yemeni's strong penchant for house design. This is primarily articulated in the architecture itself, with moldings and the selection of variously colored materials. Added to this simple or complex language, which is proof of the inventive talent of masons, is the plaster, lime, or painted outline, which sometimes looks like lace around the whole or part of the building (1 Kahil; 2 / 3 Manakha; 4 Thula region).

OPPOSITE 1
This design gives an idea of the architectural and decorative wealth that characterize northern Yemeni homes, both in villages and in cities. Correctly speaking, it is not a question of mural art, but a decorative expression tightly linked to the architecture's molding and the function of its composing elements. Here, abundant ornamentation outlined in crisp, white limewater runs along the facade like lace and embroidery.

1

1

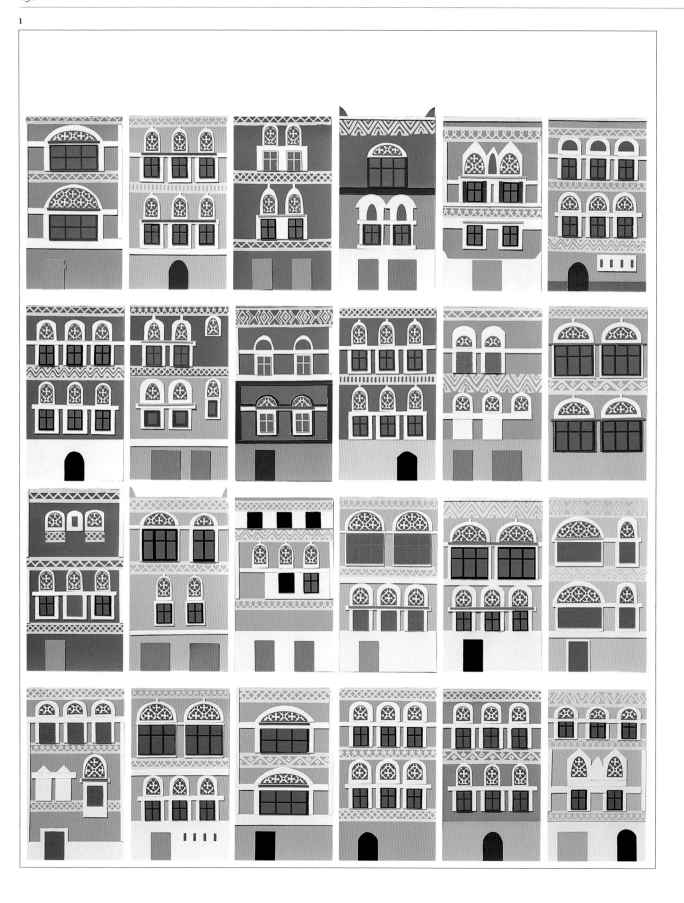

1/2
Al-Hajjara; Amran

OPPOSITE 1
Synthesis chart of North Yemen

1

2

SOUTH YEMEN

Up until independence, South Yemen was generally divided in three parts: the British colony made up of Aden and its surrounding area, the eastern protectorate or Hadramaout, and the four sultanates. Our study focused on the Hadramaout River valley, along one of the two main rivers of the Arabian peninsula. This waterway temporarily swells during the rainy season, but runs dry the rest of the year. The valley is made up of a long, verdant oasis carved between two cliffs that are the same ochre color as the ground. The agriculture of Hadramaout is connected to the rains and to irrigation, and even though fruit trees, palm trees, cotton, and wheat do grow here, the harvest is not sufficient for the countryside and it is necessary to import food.

Hadramites move away to Indonesia and Saudi Arabia to make their living, but always remain faithful to their country and come back to build large, colorful homes in bright pastel tones, as they do in Indonesia. Whether it is coated or not, the basic building material continues to be the sediment extracted from the riverbeds, which is mixed with cut straw, poured into wood framing or between two pieces of sheet metal, and compacted with a beater. With their earthen coatings, the traditional buildings have exactly the same color as the rocky mountains and when they are built up, they recall the kasbahs of southern Morocco. The musharabia and window frames are sculpted from imported Indian teak. When the landscape allows for it, free-standing dwellings are dispersed along the road, about 65 to 98 feet (20 to 30 meters) away, but for security reasons, urban constructions are preferred.

Seyun, the economic capital, Tarim, and Shibam are the three jewels of Hadramaout and it is here that the most spectacular achievements in adobe can be admired. As in northern Yemen, the houses stand several stories high and are organized in practically the same fashion; often a wall hides the entryway in order to maintain women's privacy.

The city of Seyun has much charm, with its palm trees and the seemingly disordered layout of its mosques, houses, cemeteries, and small streets through which sheep and goats wander. Twenty-two miles (35 kilometers) from Seyun, Tarim is home to a large number of mosques, 365 in fact, and houses of every style, especially luxurious Javanese-style palaces, most of which are in ruins today for lack of means to maintain them.

1

More than Seyun and Tarim, Shibam holds your attention and stirs admiration for many reasons, first for its location: in the middle of the desert, off the beaten track, it stands tall in the golden plain like a mirage, with five hundred raw-clay high-rises built on a natural, four-sided foundation and surrounded by walls. At its feet, a large expanse of blond sand pads the riverbeds and separates the old city from modern Shibam, built at the base of a cliff and along its steep sides. In order to protect against enemies, Shibam was built upward on a narrow piece of land within ramparts pierced by a single door. There are no gardens as in Sana'a, but a mineral universe of six- to seven-story tower houses, constructed very close to each other, but not flush, creating an undulating line of facades. The thickness of the walls, which gradually lessens with each floor, and the smooth appearance of the tall exteriors punctuated with narrow windows, give this architecture an ethereal quality against the backdrop of an intense blue sky.

2

1
In perfect homochromy with the surrounding mineral landscape, these three abandoned fortress-houses, between the cliff and palm grove, are an eloquent symbol of this site's aridity (Hidya).

2
Built in the sixteenth century, Shibam arranges its clay brick tower-houses along the desert sands. Through volume and the rhythm of windows, these antique skyscrapers, built tightly together within an enclosing wall, form a compact and homogeneous
architectural whole whose unity is reinforced by a chromatic palette comprising light ochres and white. The green palm trees and blue sky stand in contrast to their impermanent colors.

1

OPPOSITE 1
In southern Yemen, Wadi Hadrama-out forms a 124-mile-long (200 kilo-meter) oasis along a river swollen with the waters of the rainy season, bringing life to these desert lands (Hadra-al-Maout means "presence of death").

A general chromatic uniformity—ochre, sometimes with touches of white plaster—reinforces the impression of the exceptional homogeneity of this cityscape; only the caisson doors painted in different colors express of the occupant's whimsy.

Unfortunately, Shibam has suffered from recurring flooding and from the growth of Seyun, which is the economic seat of Hadramaout, and no longer has the means to preserve a heritage that requires constant care. Since 1982, however, this earthen masterpiece and its enclosing wall have been registered on the list of worldwide monuments.

1

1/2/3
Once you penetrate the sole entry through the ramparts, Shibam displays the density of its cityscape made up of narrow streets and small, rectangular plazas. Narrow windows with sculpted shutters accentuate the general feeling of verticality. The old, studded wood doors are the only openings at street level, as the apartments are on the floors above.

1

2

3

1 / 2 / 3 / 4 / 5 / 6 7 / 8 / 9

These doors in Tarim and vicinity are sculpted in sheet metal; the reinforcing flat bars soldered onto each section form geometric compositions, revealing Yemeni imagination and their taste for strong, contrasting colors.

1

1

1

OPPOSITE 1

In both the north and south, Yemeni architecture is remarkable for the richness of its materials. In the baking sun, you can particularly notice the strict complementarity between light, *matter, and color, and the tactile specificity of each of these masonries (1 Tarim; opposite, 1 Manakha).*

INDIA

RAJASTHAN

Situated in the northwest of India, Rajasthan is a vast state, but it is relatively unpopulated in comparison to the rest of the country, mainly because of its paucity of natural resources and its essentially desert landscape.

The state of Rajasthan owes its uniqueness to several factors, some historical, others geographical and climatic. It is laid out in the form of a diamond, crossed by the Arawalli range from north to south, with a dry plain to the west made up primarily of bushes and thorny steppes all the way to the Thar Desert along the Pakistani border, with its sand piled high in dunes. To the east is an ensemble of partially basaltic plateaus where rainfall is more abundant and the land more fertile.

1

Rajasthan's unity comes mainly from the historical importance played by the Rajputs, starting in the sixth century, after the fall of the Gupta empire. These "sons of kings," part of the Kshatriya warrior caste, formed a social and military elite at the head of their small chiefdoms, known for their legendary courage resisting the Turkish invaders, and subsequently against the Maharats, who were hoping to establish a new empire. In the early nineteenth century, the Rajputs signed treaties with the British, allowing them to maintain a certain autonomy within their states. The states disappeared with Indian liberation, but a whole list of privileges was granted to the maharajahs.

1
OPPOSITE 1
These bird's-eye views of Jaisalmer and Jodhpur, located in western Rajasthan, eloquently illustrate the concept of the geography of color. One is entirely built in yellow sandstone, the other in red sandstone that is washed in blue, each one affirming, from 124 miles (200 kilometers) away, their very special chromatic identity.

Indian political and social life is still very affected by the caste divisions inherited from Brahmanism, generally known today as Hinduism, a term that covers the diverse beliefs and popular practices of 80 percent of the population. Even though the 1950 constitution prohibited discrimination based on the caste system, the Brahmans who work in the service of temples or in fields of intellectual activity, the Kshatriya warrior caste (more numerous in Rajasthan than elsewhere), and the Vaisya caste that includes peasants and merchants, are the three "Varnas" or "colors" of the reincarnated (as initiates of Brahma's mysteries), who benefit from certain rights and privileges. In addition, the mass of Sudras includes poorer peasants and manual laborers, all divided into hundreds of castes and subcastes. On the fringe of this compartmentalized society are those who were judged to be unequal, the descendants of the indigenous inhabitants, reputed to be "impure and untouchable," who live in the worst conditions and perform the jobs that no one else will.

The population of Rajasthan is basically rural and has a relatively efficient farming economy, due in large part to the Indira Gandhi Canal, which carries water from the Himalayas all the way to the Thar Desert. Across this arid land, the people now cultivate rice, wheat, sugarcane, groundnuts, and rapeseed (India is the world's largest producer of oils), legumes (the widely consumed chick peas, beans, and lentils), millet, and cotton.

In addition, Rajasthan is a region dedicated to raising animals with livestock comprising cattle, sheep, and goats. In the desert, raising dromedaries is quite common; in these regions, it is not uncommon to see dromedaries wandering in groups, freely and calmly chewing the leaves off the trees growing along the way. Indian cars slow down, quite used to the endless crossings of all sorts of roaming animals. In the evening, dromedaries come back to their desert owners whose earthen huts are created from nature. These tall animals are used for pulling carts loaded with tree branches or sometimes large stones. White bulls are also used as draft animals.

1

From one city to the next the distance is sometimes so great that large gatherings are established in regular intervals; religious feasts, markets, and temporary commercial fairs are reasons for people to meet and exchange news and merchandise.

Smaller industries and artisanal work (spinning, weaving, pottery, goldsmithing, embroidery, ivory work, etc.) still occupy an important place in today's Rajasthani economy, even though this country remains one of the least industrialized of the Indian subcontinent. Very large, private, multi-industrial powers hold a veritable monopoly, like the automobile producer Tata which inundates the Rajasthani highways with its countless eighteen-wheelers. These orange trucks (keep in mind that orange is, along with blue and green, one of the colors of the Indian flag) are creatively personalized by their drivers, who express themselves through various designs and messages reminding people to honk before passing.

1 / 2

Jaipur, the capital city of Rajasthan, asserts its particular palette of ochre pinks with, on the one hand, the pink sandstone of its monuments, such as the famous Hawa Mahal, or Palace of the Winds, and on the other, the pink plasters that have covered the exteriors along main arteries since the visit of the future King Edward VII, in 1876. The Palace of the Winds, built a century earlier, continues to surprise and enchant with its refined proportions and elegant balconies with ornate windows.

1

1
The main arteries of the "pink city" are colored, bustling, and abundant. All types of vehicles cross these paths as well as animals as varied as camels, elephants, buffalo, and horses, under the unflinching gaze of sacred cows.

Parrots fly through the air and monkeys jump from one cornice to another. The dominant pinks and ochres are punctuated by architectural details in white, ivory, jade green, and brown.

With their stylized designs, imposing size, and sheer quantity, these vehicles are very impressive to see along the major highways where, in an endless line for miles upon miles, they sow fear. Among the sacred cows, wandering dogs, and packs of dromedaries, all witnesses to a living ancestry, these trucks are the fascinating new beasts of the modern era.

A large portion of the population lives in poverty, often quite severe poverty, since many people are unemployed. Peasants, fleeing the arid countryside, emigrate toward cities where the misery is often worse, with entire families sleeping and living on the streets. In the villages, where Gandhi saw "the true India," poverty is accepted with much dignity and with the economic and emotional support of the family, a large family containing as many as fifteen members.

Daily life is harsh here: women get up at four in the morning, fetch water from the well, grind wheat for the traditional *chappati* and *paratha* breads, clean the house, wash the dishes, and then go to work in the fields. Our young guide from Jodhpur proclaimed with admiration, "Indian woman is very strong!" Along highways and in cities, it is not uncommon to see the road being mended by women in pink or yellow saris, handling shovels like the men and carrying heavy loads, their babies resting nearby on a mound of dirt.

1

OPPOSITE 1

In Jaipur's city center, pink ochre is pervasive, while in outlying neighborhoods and on certain palaces, yellow ochre is combined in several hues. These tones, worked on by the passing time, become subtly and delicately patinated.

2

The main arteries in the "pink city" are dominated by the ochre that was imposed on residents a century ago; this dominant color comes in multiple, related tones that range from deep, red-brown to light pink. In adjacent streets, residents give free rein to their imagination, using various hues and intensities of green, yellow, and sometimes blue on their house fronts. Punctuation with carpentry, in warm-cold contrasts, brings this chromatic palette to life. This chart was made in January 1996.

1

2

3

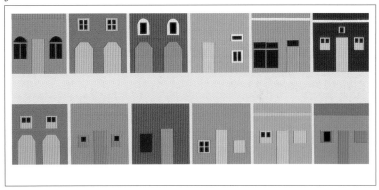

4

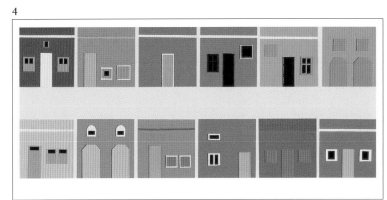

3/4

These vignettes, simplifying the facades analyzed on site, are placed in the same order as they are found along Jaipur's narrow streets.

1

2

3

1

Most families in villages and in the country own the home that they live in. The most modest homes have one or two rooms; the more stylish homes have four or five, situated around a sort of patio, a corner of which is used as the kitchen. Under thatched roofs, the walls of rural homes are generally built with a mix of clay, straw, and cow dung, to which pieces of stone are added to make the structure more solid. Solidly built homes bear witness to a more elevated social and economic status and are a sign of prosperity; their rooms are laid out in the same way as their more modestly constructed counterparts.

Rajasthanis are artists. Their sense of color and aesthetic as well as their decorative arts permeate every aspect of daily life: clothes, jewelry, utilitarian pottery, diverse artisanry, interior and exterior home design, and the stylized patterns painted on vehicles, bulls' horns, even elephants! The home, protected by the goddess Lakshmi, is at the heart of almost every social and ritual gathering in India. Every year, during Dipavali, the goddess's festival for weddings and baptisms, women repaint their homes and decorate them with patterns that vary according to the region. Ganesh, the god with the head of an elephant, son of Siva and Parvati, is depicted on every house where a wedding has been celebrated to bring luck and prosperity to the newlyweds. The walls of homes and enclosures are also painted with palm trees, tigers, elephants, and mythical scenes.

In Rajasthan, traditional dress for women is quite colorful; it consists of a large skirt that is gathered at the waist (*ghaghara*), a small, richly embroidered blouse or bolero vest (*kurti-kanchli*), and a veil (*odhani*) that allows them to cover their shoulders and head as well as hide their faces. These light clothes, floating in graceful movements with every step, are bright in tonalities, with daring blends of reds and pinks, saffrons, and yellows, blues, and greens, which "sing" gaily and resound in infinite combinations, the colors varying according to caste and location. In the desert, women wrap themselves in tie-dyed veils with patterns and colors that have specific meanings, and after the birth of an heir, they wear a *peeliya*, a yellow robe with red patterning. Men have a more moderate style of dress: a certain number have adopted European-style pants, but most remain faithful to the *dhoti*, which wraps through the legs and ties in the back at the waist, generally worn with a long, white shirt. The only spray of color comes from a brightly colored turban.

2

3

OPPOSITE 1/2/3
This urban landscape dominated by pink ochre is enlivened with a selective palette of ivory, jade green, and brown tones on carpentry work and with a white line that traces the molding around the facade. The lengthy shadows add their impermanent colors to this palette and accentuate the architecture's rhythmic language.

1/2/3
Architecture in Jaipur and its surrounding areas offers a wide variety of ochre tones, from yellow to red ochre, passing through diverse degrees of saturation and lightness. Iron oxide, the base pigment for these tones, gives them an overall visual coherence as a landscape.

1

2

3

4

1 / 2 / 3 / 4
In the old section of the city, small streets line a pedestrian area where different color registers appear: the general palette of untreated or painted yellow sandstone, the selective palette of doors, windows, frames, and foundations, and the random colors represented here by the lively saris.

As for the color of homes, when it is a shelter made of local soil or sand, they are perfectly harmonious with their natural environment to the point of almost completely melting into them. Pure color is more visible in cities where homes are built in brick and red, yellow, or pink limestone; exteriors are left in their original material, or are plastered and covered in paint: pink ochre in Jaipur, blue in Jodhpur.

JAIPUR: THE PINK CITY

Jaipur takes its name from its founder, Sawai Jai Singh II, one of the most remarkable men of his time: a brilliant military leader, a respected politician, and an intellectual taken with art and astronomy. In November 1727, he decided to leave the narrow Amber Pass to erect a city worthy of his name (*jai* means victory), out on a plain at the edge of a parched lake.

Through this undertaking, Jai Singh II proved to be a particularly astute urban planner; he decided that his city would be the first Rajput city drawn on a grid, with wide, perpendicular avenues creating residential blocks. His desire was to see this city become the Rajput capital. His dream was realized, and since the Indian independence, Jaipur, with two million residents (including those that live in the surrounding area), has become the administrative and economic capital of Rajasthan.

1

1

In the heart of the Thar Desert, in the westernmost part of Rajasthan, Jaisalmer, which is built in yellow sandstone, is rightly called the "golden city." From one of the terraces of Patwon Ki Haveli, you can see the *exquisite finesse of sculpted ornaments and the architectural elegance of these palaces that were erected in the nineteenth century by wealthy merchants.*

Jaipur is a very lively city with heavy traffic, a tangle of every type of vehicle: trucks, fancy cars, taxis, scooters, bicycles, rickshaws, pedal carts, carts pulled by cattle or dromedaries, all swarming in a deafening scream of horns under the peaceful gaze of the numerous sacred animals seeking refuge on sidewalks and the narrow central medians of the avenues. Beside cows, bulls, and camels, roaming dogs and even pigs scurry through pedestrians' legs, while monkeys gently climb along houses where green parrots perch. Out of a basket on the ground, a magnificent cobra suddenly emerges, drawn by the sound of its owner's flute. With all of these animals, Jaipur is a true Noah's Ark, which is one of the most fascinating aspects of this bustling city!

The countless small shops, with their wonders piled high, are another—multicolored spices, enticing fabrics, cooking utensils in terra-cotta and white iron, and Sulpician images of mythological heroes.

The "pink city" owes its name primarily to the color of the public monuments built by Jai Singh in red sandstone, such as the City Palace, a royal palace composed of a whole chain of palaces, temples, and gardens. The Hawa Mahal, or Palace of the Winds, built in 1799, is a stunning five-story, honeycombed facade, barely a room deep! This airy sculpture, though monumental, was designed so that women of the court could attend public gatherings without being seen, hidden behind the intricate musharabia screens of the bay balconies. It was not until the following century that the whole city was painted in pink, as a sign of welcome, in 1876, for the future King Edward VII. Public leaders keep close watch on the upkeep of these pink-ochre facades (at least on the main streets) and ramparts surrounding the city, giving the capital city of Rajasthan an exceptional architectural and chromatic unity.

1

1/2/3

OPPOSITE 1

Ganesh, the god with the head of an elephant, brings prosperity and luck to young couples; he consequently adorns the exteriors of homes where weddings are celebrated. In addition, around entryways, women paint sacred patterns passed on to them by their mothers and created in honor of Lakshmi, the protectress of home and family.

252

1

*Sandstone as well as ochre and golden
yellow plaster make up the principal
chromatics of the general palette, while
the selective palette is mainly
illustrated with green, blue, and
turquoise tones.*

*Both harmonious and spontaneous,
this spectrum recorded in 1996 conveys
Indians' innate sense of color.*

JAISALMER

Jaisalmer is located in the Thar Desert, the "land of
death," not far from the Pakistani border. Little by
little, this pebbly countryside, dotted with shrubs
and a few trees, turns into vast, sandy expanses
called *dharna*; without plant life, its shape shifts
with the winds. Cultivating plants is rare here and
is mainly done during the wet season when millet,
lentils, and sesame can be grown. Here and there,
rapeseed is grown, along with a little barley and
wheat in the valleys.

The district of Jaisalmer has been transformed over
the past few years by the construction of the Indira
Gandhi Canal, bringing water from the Himalayas
to the Thar Desert; the main section was completed
on January 1, 1987. The pandit Nehru's dream of
taming these arid steppes with water has now been
realized. Raising sheep, goats, and camels also
contribute to the wealth of the region's tribes. The
camels of Jaisalmer are famous for their rhythmic
step and resilience, and are highly coveted by
people in the desert who take great care of them.
The Rajput Rawal Jaisal, on the advice of an old
hermit, founded the citadel of Jaisalmer in 1156.
Built in yellow sandstone, on the slopes of Tricuta,
the city displays a stunning homochromy with the
surrounding desert sands. Despite its isolation, it is
rapidly becoming wealthier from the high taxes
imposed on caravans following the spice trail
toward Delhi. During the eighteenth and
nineteenth centuries, the wealthy merchants had
sumptuous *havelis* built, with yellow sandstone
exteriors as intricate as lace. The delicately sculpted
stone screens let air through and allow women to
see without being seen, thereby gaining access to
the show on the street. The sculptor's genius shines
through in countless floral and geometric patterns
that stir admiration.

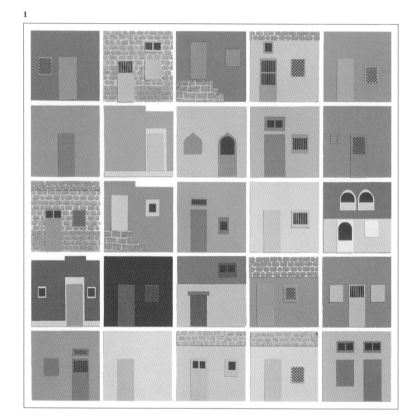

1

2

After the British opened up the ports of Bombay and Calcutta and the trade routes disappeared, Jaisalmer gradually lost all contact with the outside world and residents left the city to seek their fortunes elsewhere. Today, the city has been reinvigorated by modern transportation and the development of its tourist industry.

The city of Jaisalmer is exceptional for the chromatic unity of its yellow sandstone, for the quality of the architecture, whether havelis or simple residential homes within the citadel, and for the magical atmosphere that emanates from these history-laden walls.

1

1

OPPOSITE 2
On modest dwellings, coatings of ochre soil recall the yellow sand of the Thar Desert.

The vibrant structure of these annually renewed surfaces is often brightened with selective elements designed in crisp, white limewater.

JODHPUR

Jodhpur, located on the eastern edge of the Thar Desert, is Rajasthan's second major city in importance and population. Initially called Jodhagarh, or the "land of Jodha," it was founded in 1459 by Rao Jodha, who came from the clan of Rajputs, said to be descendants of the sun. At the time, Rao Jodha was the sovereign of Mandore, 5 miles (8 kilometers) away, but heeding the wise advice of a hermit, he established his capital city in the secure heights of a sandstone hill from where he would be able to look out over his entire kingdom. In fact, from atop the Mehrangarh fort, encircled and protected by a fortified wall 6 miles (10 kilometers) long, the view over the blue city is exceptional. The old houses are in fact built with local materials, pink sandstone or the softer red sandstone, which were easy to cut and shape, but most have been coated and painted in blue indigo. According to our Indian guide, the custom of painting Jodhpur's houses blue dates back to the sixteenth century; at that time, it was a tradition of the Brahman class to allow the maharajah to identify their homes from the fort above. Today, blue houses are quite numerous and, even though Brahman homes are always blue, blue houses are not necessarily Brahman homes.

2

1

1
Sandstone masonry sealed with a thick layer of mortar takes on an impressive relief in the searing morning heat.

The remarkable texture of this bas-relief gives life to the intense blue that is characteristic of the old neighborhoods of Jodhpur.

2
From atop Fort Mehrangarh in Jodhpur, the city's bluish fabric of terraced homes spreads out into the distance.

Added to the dominant range of various, intense blues, touches of red sandstone and beige plaster of newer homes dot the city.

1

1
The old Brahman quarter, built in the sixteenth century, is annually repainted in intense cobalt blue for the feast of Divali. Sculpted and decorated corbels, balconies, terraces, and balustrades create a flurry of architectural detail that work with the individual "language" of each house, even the most modest.

The penchant here for blue has several explanations: one is that Jodhpur is an extremely sunny city and blue reflects the sun less than white; this color also helps to keep away mosquitoes; and in the end, the residents simply have a fondness for indigo.

It should also be noted that blue is the color of Krishna, the god of love. On facades, near the doorway, it is common to find hand-painted designs: flowers, palm trees, animals, and the heroes of Hindu mythology. Sacred cows wander peacefully through the calm and narrow streets.

For more recent homes, people now prefer pink sandstone, because for them, according to our guide, "it seems newer and cleaner;" stone houses and palisades painted in pink ochre, which is, along with blue, a favored color for the residents in Jodhpur, can also be found.

1

1

OPPOSITE 1 / 2 / 3 / 4
The old city of Jodhpur is remarkable for the quality and refinement of its complex architecture, decorated with angles and sculptures.

Against the dominant blues of the general palette, green carpentry contrasts strongly, while still remaining in the cooler register of colors.

1

2

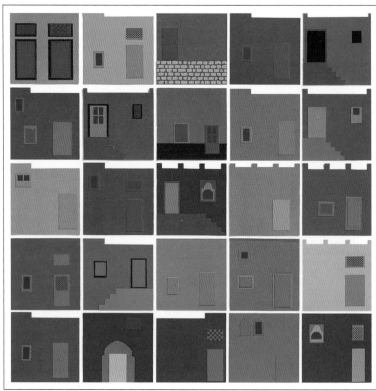

3

1/3
This group of homes, in the characteristic colors of Jodhpur's old quarters, was first photographed from afar, and then up close. These snapshots illustrate the concepts of global and elemental perspective, developed in the chapter about site color analysis.

2
The twenty-five vignettes assembled here outline the colors of old Jodhpur. Among the dominant blues, a few ochre and red sandstone tones are an exception to the rule. The selective palette is almost exclusively made up of green tones that range from yellow-green to turquoise, in every shade of brightness (1996).

OPPOSITE 1
Pink, yellow, and blue: these are the emblematic colors of Jaipur, Jaisalmer, and Jodhpur. While Jaisalmer, which is built in yellow sandstone, has a completely golden surface, Jaipur is pink in the city center and along main arteries; Jodhpur is mainly blue within the confines of the neighborhood where Brahmans live.

1

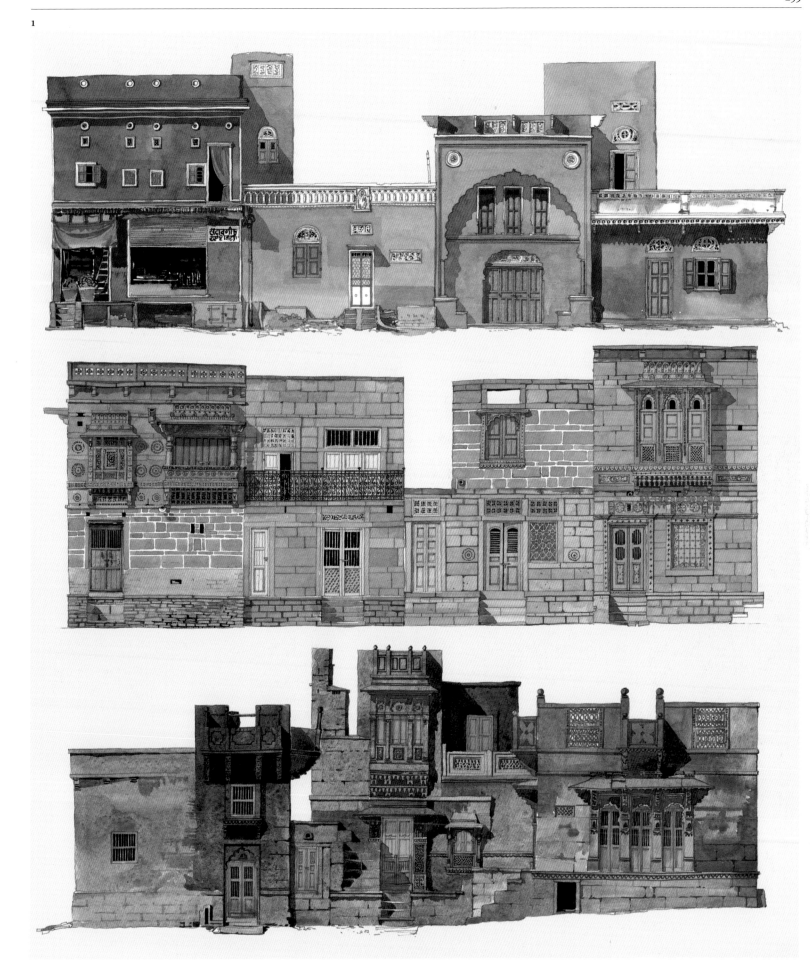

THE THAR DESERT

In the desert regions along the Pakistani border, the camel herders' wives decorate their low, earthen houses once a year with bold geometric figures, for Dipavali, the festival of Lakshmi.

These prayers to the goddess of the home are a stunning and ephemeral reminder of the humble homes that melt into the surrounding desert, both in their color and materials.

1

1 / 2 / 3
OPPOSITE 1
In the Thar Desert along Pakistan, random villages melt into the landscape's blond sand, with earthen walls and roofs made from plant life. Here, color is also substance; the elemental perspective allows us to measure the subtlety of relief and texture of walls coated in a mix of soil and camel dung to prevent against crumbling and lizards (Khuri).

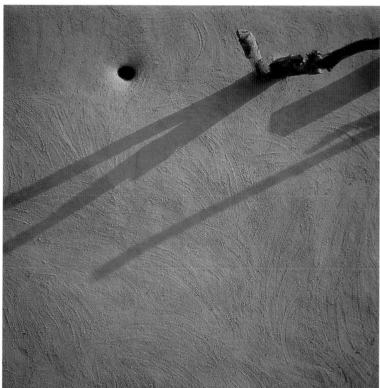

1

2

1 / 2 / 3 / 4
OPPOSITE 1 / 2
Every year, during the Dipavali season, camel herders' wives decorate their homes with geometric patterns to honor Lakshmi, the goddess of fortune and prosperity.

These traditional designs are passed from mother to daughter and range from simple abstractions to more narrative expressions (Khuri).

JAPAN

MUROTSU

Murotsu is a small fishing port on Japan's interior coast, located to the east of Kobe. It was one of several cities that, having long been established along maritime trade routes, experienced a period of great prosperity in the seventeenth century, as is still evident by the presence of several homes that belonged to wealthy merchants. At that time, Murotsu was a city of about eight hundred houses, which reflected the importance of this port so naturally carved into the mountain landscape. Yet, two hundred years later, with the development of highway and rail transportation, a gradual decline has gripped this ancient city, a city so highly regarded since the twelfth century that it was honored with the construction of the Kamo Jinja temple, an extension of the Kamo Jinja temple in the imperial city of Kyoto.

1

The name *Murotsu* is formed from the words "bedroom" and "shelter," which shows how much security this naturally protected enclave, surrounded by mountains, afforded to travelers.

Murotsu has now been incorporated into the city of Mitsucho, comprising its fishing harbor and historic district, and basically consists of one main artery that is home to a population of fifteen hundred residents.

The town is a homogeneous ensemble of old homes from the Edo period, practically representative of traditional Japanese homes. A few adjoining streets have more recent buildings whose proportions match the older style.

1

1
OPPOSITE 1
Murotsu is a fishing port near the historic city of Himeji, on Japan's interior coastline. Professor Shingo Yoshida, who appreciated its homogeneity and authentic character, *guided us to our selection of this city. What is remarkable about the traditional Japanese architecture here is that its quality is apparent in the overall urban landscape as well as in the smallest details.*

1

1

Nestled in a natural bay surrounded by mountains, dwellings in Murotsu appear, seen here from above, allowing us to discover the particular "language" of Japanese roofs in varnished tiles. The governing color scale, established *in 1995, suggests relatively dark grays for roof materials.*

1

1 / 2
These snapshots of Murotsu's port capture a certain atmosphere: the patinated woods, the gray roof tiles spotted with silver, and the light plasters create a palette of muted colors that characterizes the charm of everyday Japanese dwellings. A few colored accents punctuate spaces here and there, whether the blue or red-brown of roofs or the random colors that come from activity in the harbor. Note how the fishing boats are as somber in color as the homes lining the docks.

2

1

2

Traditional Japanese architecture is primarily constructed from plant-life materials. Even if there is recourse to the soil for tiles and cob, wood is used first and foremost—wood was the only building material used until the Meiji period—since it is abundant, easy to work with, and particularly well adapted to the country's climate. The types of wood that are most often used are resin woods such as cedar, pine, cypress, and fir. Traditional construction also uses mulberry paper to cover sliding windows, or *shoji*, and bamboo, which is used to build wooden slats. Together, all of these materials help integrate the house smoothly into the surrounding countryside; in addition, they deteriorate, which means that they are in perfect harmony with the Japanese taste for the ephemeral, and the culture's belief in the impermanence of beings and things.

The use of wood imposes certain constraints, particularly the need for modest proportions. The framework is a simple structure, consisting of a skeleton of vertical and horizontal sections connected together to support the roof. This structure stands on stones, but there are no foundations as there are in Western homes. Overall, stone is rarely used, and architectural proportions are dictated by the sections of *tatami*, the basic component of traditional homes.

1

1

OPPOSITE 1 / 2
The older residences, located along the main street, summarize the characteristic elements of traditional urban architecture from the Meiji period: scale and proportion, wood, the dominant material of the facade, gray-tile roofing, and a general palette of somber colors.

Today, Murotsu has municipal ordinances governing material and color choice, and certain homes are part of the city's historic and cultural heritage.

1

1

Along the main street, the Jakujho-Ji, one of Murotsu's many temples, is flanked by a residential home, seen here, where the monk in charge of the temple lives. Recently restored according to the rules of its art, this residence displays its original resin colors, not yet darkened by time's patina. Between the framing pillars, sections of the facade that are not dressed in wooden planks are finely smoothed with white plaster. With its walkways in granite flagstone lined with clay, the mineral tones of the courtyard act as a counterpoint to the overall wood construction.

1

1

The view across the cemetery next to the Tokujho-Ji temple. The dark, baked clay of the molded roofs and the intense green of the vegetation constitute the dominant colors of the landscape.

1

The roof, whose name means "root of the house," is high and massive, and is of great visual importance. It can have the most varied forms and, depending on the region and the residents' means, is covered with reeds, rice or wheat straw, shingles or tiles. Among tiles, there is a difference between *hongawara*, comparable to Roman tile, which was used in the seventeenth century; *sangawara*, or gently crocheted tile; and *kawara*, which is formed like waves and recalls Flemish roof moldings. The tile's grayish color comes from the carbon that forms on clay during the final stages of firing.

Walls are made up of bamboo trellises attached to wood pillars, coated with a varnish made of clay and straw which is then varnished again. The lateral walls of traditional homes are often completely covered over with gently overlapping planks, or shitamiita. The natural wood walls take on a patina over time, or are tinted black; if they are coated, they are often painted white or dark gray. This type of architectural layout gives an impression of sobriety, balance, and harmony in strict accord with the environment.

1/2

OPPOSITE 1

Cedar, pine, cypress, and fir are the most frequent resin woods used for construction. The warm, brown tones of the wooden latticework, or kushi, *that protects the paper windows take on a particular quality in contrast to the white* shoji. *The facade's modular language reminds us that tatami is the basic element that serves as a measuring tool. In the photo at right, the bamboo shade, or* sudare, *rounds out the palette of plant materials.*

1

The mountainous terrain into which the city is implanted creates vistas overlooking the tile roofs framed by vegetation.

The range of baked-clay roofing joins with the palette of plasters and wood coverings to form a homogeneous chromatic ensemble of muted colors.

1
Another way to approach the urban complexity of Murotsu is through its small streets where you see the tangle of telephone and electrical wires, which are left exposed in case of seismic activity.

The sobriety of colors and the asserted rhythms of the landscape's various components create a pictorial composition that is quite representative of smaller Japanese cities.

1

2

3

4

1 / 2 / 3 / 4

OPPOSITE 1

*Analyzing a site's chromatic details
shows how permanent elements—
flooring, walls, roofs, architectural
elements—are enriched by the
proliferation of selective, impermanent, and random elements.*

With their roofs covered in kawara and walls that take on a patina from the wind and rain, the old homes of Murotsu closely follow traditional outlines. The most notable difference, which is due to an uneven mountain terrain that is specifically suited to construction, is that most homes have only a single level. Along the street, the facades continue in succession, giving this urban ensemble a unity that no element disturbs. The surface of the wood walls are sometimes carbonized with a blow-torch for better protection against insects and worms; they have, therefore, a deep black color to them and are soft, satiny to the touch. In certain homes, paper windows are lined with hermetic glass.

1

2

2
This synthesizing chart, made from Murotsu's residential colors, summarizes in twenty-five vignettes the three main types of architecture found in this small city: the older residences where gray roofs and somber tones of patinated wood dominate; more recent architecture, still influenced by traditional choices of material and color; and finally, the semi-industrial constructions with the new colors of their roofing material, casings, and carpentry.

1

1
In Murotsu's architecture, as well as in surrounding areas, wooden planks protecting the frame and cob are treated against insects by a process (yaki-ita) consisting of charring the surface.

The various black qualities obtained from this technique and the structure of the wood's veins and knots take on a pictorial dimension.

1
These wavelike tiles, or kawara, reminiscent of Flemish purlins, are mainly used today in individual homes.

In Murotsu, gray is the dominant color, as is recommended by the governing color chart.

1

Today, here and there, enamel-tiled roofs are starting to appear; their coloration is a move away from the traditional family of grays, with reddish-browns, blues, greens, and sometimes yellow oxides. The leap toward colored enamel tiles has been visible for the past thirty years with the arrival in Japan of countless single-home plots of land. And the colored roofs quickly catch the eye of foreigners crossing the countryside by train or plane.

In 1995, the cityscape of Murotsu was the focus of an overall color design led by the colorist Shingo Yoshida and the Color Planning Center of Tokyo, in which a range of colors was recommended for roofs, whose tonalities ranged from medium gray to black. For exteriors, the surfaces that were not made of natural wood were covered in white or light, sand-colored washes.

The selective palette is visually quite important. The visible structure of the wooden-post frame and the carpentry around bays and entryways (traditionally done in wood, but often replaced nowadays with glazed or anodized aluminum that imitates the wooden tones of yesteryear) create a steady, rhythmic flow around its coated surfaces.

1

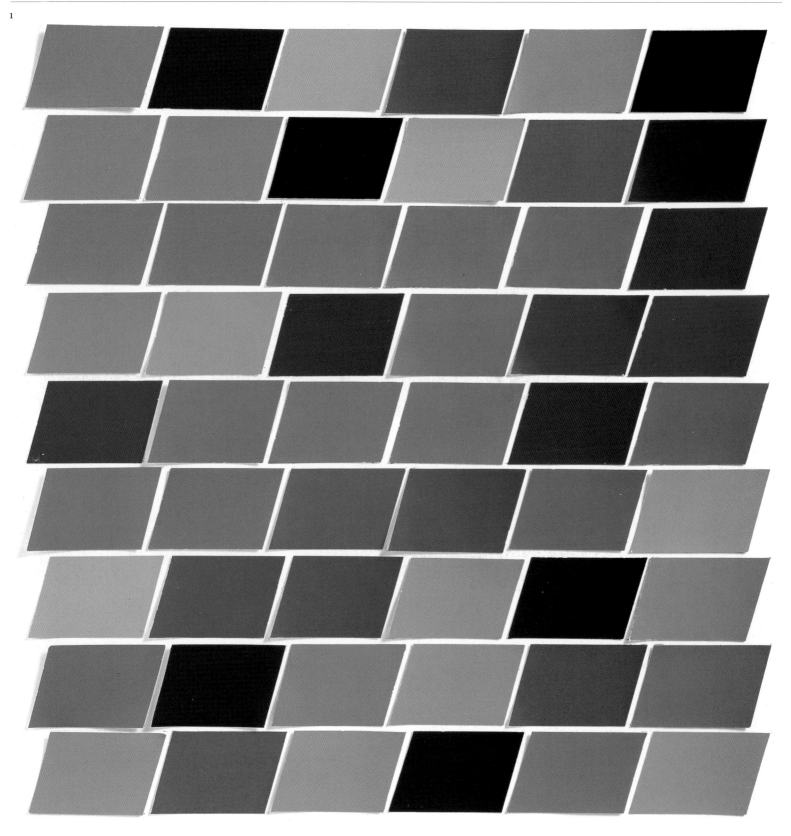

1
This spectrum of fifty-four roof colors, catalogued in Murotsu in 1997, attempts to reconstruct and simplify the chromatic climate that personalizes the general palette for roofs, largely dominated by gray and punctuated here and there, in a poetic and lively fashion, by a few touches of blue and brown.

1

2

3

4

1 / 2 / 3 / 4
These four roofs in Murotsu express
the beauty of the rhythm, form, color,
and substance of a traditional material
that is prevalent across all of Japan.
The gray roof with silver glints sits
atop the Tokujho-Ji temple.

Very popular in the seventeenth
century, this tile, hongawara, whose
rounded forms evoke Roman tiles, is
regularly used for temple roofing.

1

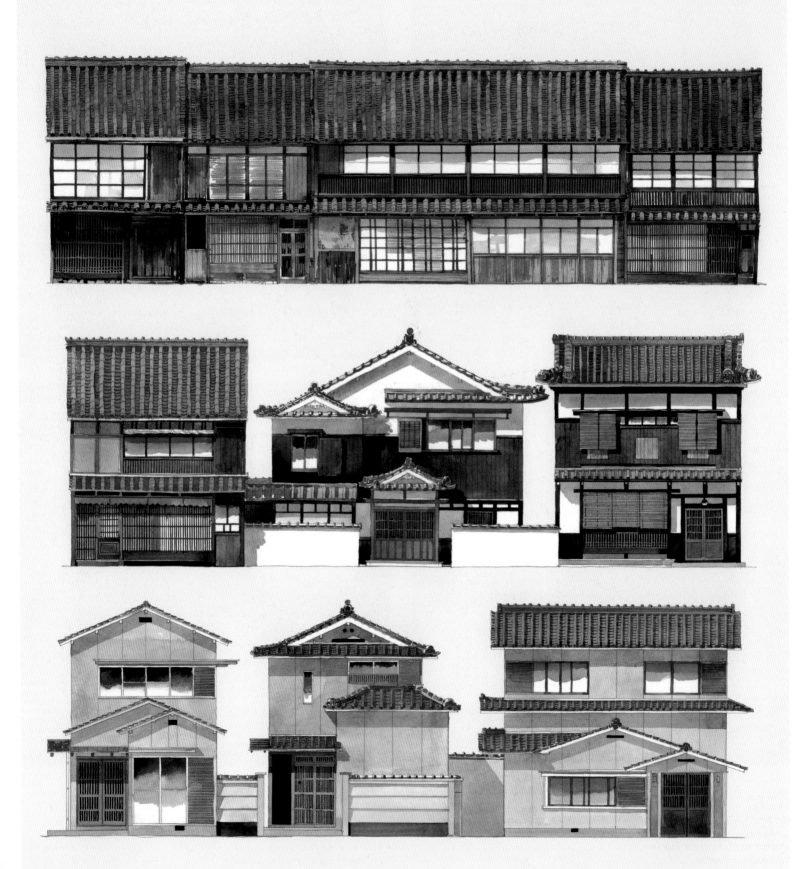

1

OPPOSITE 1
This chart of watercolor illustrations presents three types of dwellings that can be found today in Murotsu: above, a row of residences that date back to the nineteenth century and are protected on the national heritage register; in the center, more recent homes show a respect for tradition in their molding and facades; below, three modern homes where industrial building techniques are blended into a classic language.

1
These tile fragments were collected from a roofing business a few miles from Murotsu. Older tile bits demonstrate the flat, gray quality of baked clays from the past; newer tiles are generally enameled.

Even with gray as Murotsu's recommended color, you still find different tinges of blue, green, yellow ochre, and brown, all of which are colors that have become widespread for use on private homes over the past twenty years.

BOOKS, ARTICLES, AND PUBLICATIONS RELATED TO THE WORK OF JEAN-PHILIPPE LENCLOS

1967	*L'Architecture d'aujourd'hui* no. 134 (France)	"Auditorium"
	L'Express no. 9, Oct. 15 (France)	"L'utile se mesure à l'insolite" (Alice Morgaine)
1968	*Domus* no. 459 (Italy)	"Colori a Parigi"
	L'Oeil no. 159 (France)	"Auditorium"
	Elle no. 1178 (France)	"Pour tromper les murs"
1969	*Domus* no. 471 (Italy)	"Grafica per una industria"
	Connaissance des arts no. 209 (France)	"L'art et la musique"
	Les Nouvelles littéraires no. 2183 (France)	"La meilleure palette" (Gilles de Bure)
	La Maison de Marie-Claire no. 29 (France)	"La maison à vos couleurs" (Marielle Hucliez)
	Créé no. 1 (France)	"La couleur et ses déclinaisons"
	L'Express no. 936 (France)	"Les coloristes soignent à la couleur" (Alice Morgain)
1970	*Mainichi-Shinbun* (Japan)	"Environment and color"
	Color Communication no. 12 (Japan)	"The world of Jean-Philippe Lenclos"
	Housing and Urban Development (Japan)	
	Domus no. 492 (Italy)	"La couleur est un signal"
	Graphic Design no. 40 (Japan)	"Works by Jean-Philippe Lenclos"
	La Maison de Marie-Claire no. 38 (France)	"Apprenez la couleur avec les peintres" (Marielle Hucliez)
1971	*Réalités* no. 300 (France)	"L'explosion de la couleur crue" (Jean Clay)
	Approach (Japan)	"Volume—Light—Color" (Jean-Philippe Lenclos)
	The Kindaï Kenchitu no. 25 (Japan)	"Super Graphic" (Ryoichi Shigeta)
	La Maison de Marie-Claire no. 56 (France)	"Vivre en couleur"
	Créé no. 10 (France)	"Volume-couleur" (Gilles de Bure)
1972	*Color Planning Center* no. 32 (Japan)	"Lenclos the Colorist" (Masaomi Unagami)
	L'architecture d'aujourd'hui no. 164 (France)	"Couleurs et paysages" (Jean-Philippe Lenclos)
	Color Communication CPC no. 29 (Japan)	"Color Scheme of Interior Decoration" (Masaomi Unagami)
	Japan Interior Design no. 156 (Japan)	"How French Designs Have Changed"
	Asahi-Shinbun (Japan)	"La couleur de Tokyo vue par un Parisien"
	Yomiuri-Shinbun (Japan)	"A Tokyo, plus de couleur"
	Nippon Keizai-Shinbun (Japan)	"La couleur de Tokyo est gris-rose"
1973	*La Maison de Marie-Claire* no. 74 (France)	"Les matériaux naturels de la couleur"
	L'architecture d'aujourd'hui no. 166 (France)	"Aujourd'hui l'école"
	Elle no. 1424 (France)	"L'avenir des meubles: faire partie des murs" (Jacqueline Chaumont)
	Elle no. 1427 (France)	"La couleur au tableau d'honneur—Espace couleur"
	Domus no. 522 (Italy)	"Supergraphisme"
	Varisilmä no. 3 (Finland)	"Eläma on väriä"
	Abitare no. 117 (Italy)	"Viaggiare Meglio"
	Créé no. 23 (France)	"Aspen 1973" (Gilles de Bure)
	Architecture Plus no. 9 (United States)	"The Powerful Hum of Color"
1974	*La Maison de Marie-Claire* no. 85 (France)	"Choisissez vos couleurs"
	Maison Française no. 276(287 (France)	"Les Couleurs de la France" (Solange Gorce)
	Domicile no. 3 (France)	"La couleur est déjà au pouvoir" (Marianne Fell)
	Design, Editions Stock-Chêne (France)	"Introduction à l'histoire du design" (Jocelyn de Noblet)
	Domus no. 537 (Italy)	"Policromia—Les Maradas"
	Graphic Design of the World no. 7, Kodansha (Japan)	"Graphics in Environment"
	Form no. 10 (Sweden)	"Grafisk formgiving"
1975	*Mäleri* no. 2 (Sweden)	"Livet är enlek med färger"
	Le Journal de la maison no. 85 (France)	"Jean-Philippe Lenclos" (Catherine Ardouin)
	Decorativnoie Iskusstvo no. 29 (Soviet Union)	"La palette des villes françaises" (L. Jadova)
	Color Planning Center no. 62 (Japan)	"La couleur du Vaudreuil"
	GQ no. 45 (United States)	"Getting Personal: Paris Matchless"
	Elle no. 1558 (France)	"Nos trente ans"
1976	*Neuf* no. 59 (Belgium)	"Le bonheur polychrome" (Georges Durand)
	Colour for Architecture, Studio Vista (Great Britain)	"Living in Colour" (Porter and Mikellides)
	Neuf no. 63 (Belgium)	"Couleurs et architecture" (Georges Durand)
	Créé no. 42 (France)	"L'amélioration du patrimoine récent" (Gérard Negreanu)
	L'Architecture en URSS no. 6	"L'architecture contemporaine en France" (Nicolas Solovief)
1977	*Domus* no. 568 (Italy)	"Solmer—La Ciotat"
	Color Planning Center no. 76 (Japan)	"Color Environment in Europe" (Shingo Yoshida)
	AIA, American Institute of Architecture no. 67 (United States)	"Color in Architecture"
	Les Nouvelles littéraires no. 2589 (France)	"Couleurs du paysage" (Jean-François Dhuys)
	Le Point no. 263 (France)	"Celui par qui la couleur arrive" (Catherine Bergeron)
	Marie-France no. 261 (France)	"A chaque région sa couleur" (Sabine Chadenet)
	Japan Interior Design no. 233 (Japan)	"Color Scheme in Architecture" (Ryoichi Shigeta, Masaomi Unagami)
	TPE no. 44 (France)	"Les couleurs de la ville"
	Monuments historiques no. 5 (France)	"La géographie de la couleur" (Jean-Philippe Lenclos)
1978	*100 Idées* no. 51 (France)	"Nature morte: Paysage vivant" (Jean-Jacques Mandelle)
	Odia (Portugal)	"Geografia da cor"
	Woon Signatur (Netherlands)	"Arts décoratifs"
	Architecture intérieure—Créé no. 165 (France)	"Les quatre temps" (Olivier Boissière)
1979	*Car Styling* no. 25 (Japan)	"Le style automobile à la régie Renault" (Giancarlo Perini)
	Architecture intérieure—Créé no. 171 (France)	"La méthode du rhythme et des tonalités" (Patrice Goulet)
	Makasini no. 7 (Finland)	"Sopusointu on tu levaisuuden Avainsana" (Marja Paasonen)
	100 Idées no. 71 (France)	"Derrière la porte des écoles d'art" (M. Bailhache)
	Estado de Minas no 11-79 (Brazil)	"Artes visuais" (Gelma Alvim)
1980	*Domus* no. 602 (Italy)	"Colore e Torino"
	Graphic Design for Our Environment, Shotenkenchikusha Co. Ltd. (Japan)	"Rythmes de facades à Château-Double (Takenobu Igarashi)
	L'Usine Nouvelle (France)	"La couleur à l'usine"
	Japan Interior Design no. 261 (Japan)	"The Designers of the World Are Now"
	Epoca no. 1574 (Italy)	"Il colore che va" (A. Militello)
1981	*Farbe im Stadtbild*, Archibook, Berlin (Germany)	"L'aciérie Somer," "La ville nouvelle du Vaudreuil" (M. Duttmann)
	Les Couleurs dans l'architecture du Limousin, Typographica	Direction Régionale de l'Equipement du Limousin (Jean-Philippe Lenclos)

1982	*Colour Outside,* Architectural Press, London (Great Britain) (Tom Porter)	
	Les Nouvelles littéraires no. 2856 (France)	"Des murs et des couleurs" (Jean-François Dhuys)
	Light, Color, and Environment, Van Nostrand Reinhold (United States)	"The Use of Color on Exteriors" (Faber Birren)
	La Ristrutturazione edilizia, Hoepli (Italy)	"Il colore nella riabilitazione" (A. Baglioni, G. Guarnerio)
1983	*Monuments historiques* no. 129 (France)	"Des matériaux traditionnels de construction" (Henri Bonnemazou)
1984	*Le Livre du mur peint,* Alternatives (France)	"Le mur art de la rue" (Dominique Durand)
	Éléments de design industriel, Maloine (France)	"Composantes esthétiques du produit" (Danielle Quarante)
1985	*Le Point* no. 2405 (France)	"Couleurs: la palette des sens" (Roselyne Bosch)
	Color Model Environments, Van Nostrand Reinhold (United States)	"The Work of Jean-Philippe Lenclos" (Harold Linton)
1986	*Automobiles classiques* no. 15 (France)	"Couleurs et matières du futur" (Serge Bellu)
	Paris tête d'affiche no. 3 (France)	"La nouvelle Nouvelle Athènes" (Philippe Lavorel)
	La France sensible, Champ Vallon (France)	"La France et ses couleurs" (Pierre Sansot)
1987	*L'Express* no. 1488 (France)	"Les villes sont des palettes" (Odile Perrard)
	Paris Passion no. 52 (France)	"The Heavy 100" (Marion Tompkins)
	Diagonal no. 66 (France)	"La couleur comme des racines" (Florence Marot)
	Le Monde "affaires" no. 13340	"Les marchands de couleurs" (Christian Tortel)
1988	*Maison française* no. 414 (France)	"Le monde en technicolor" (Inès Heugel)
	Tools no. IV/3 (Denmark)	"United Colors of Lenclos"
	Encyclopedia of Architecture, John Wiley (United States)	"Color in Architecture" (Tom Porter)
	Car Styling nos. 64, 65, 66, 67, 68 San'ei Shobo Publishing Co., Ltd. (Japan)	"The Geography of Color" (Akira, Fujimoto)
	Le Rêve automobile, EPA (France)	"Atelier 3D Couleur" (Serge Bellu, Peter Vann)
1989	*Today* (China)	"Un Français maître de la couleur" (Song Jian Ming)
	The Color Compendium, Van Nostrand Reinhold (United States)	"Architecture and Color" (Augustine Hope, Margaret Walch)
	Intramuros no. 25 (France)	"Jean-Philippe Lenclos" (Claudine Farrugia)
	Journal of Zheijang Academy of Fine Arts (China)	"Jean-Philippe Lenclos: Method for Teaching the Colors" (Song Jian Ming)
	Signs and Structures, Akzo Coatings (Netherlands)	"The Geography of Color" (Jean-Philippe Lenclos)
	Le Point no. 888 (France)	"Un homme de couleurs" (Guillemette de Sairigné)
1990	*Maison française* no. 436 (France)	"Au pays de la couleur" (Claude Berthod)
	City no. 60	"Cités polychromes" (Renaud Ego)
	Philips News no. 9 (Holland)	"Colour scheme for new range designed by Jean-Philippe Lenclos"
	La Couleur de la ville no. 2 (Russia)	"Geography of colour" (Andrei Efimov)
1991	*Car Styling* no. 80 (Japan)	"At the salon de Paris" (Jean-Philippe Lenclos)
	Figaro no. 14429 (France)	"Jean-Philippe Lenclos docteur ès couleur" (Chantal de Rosamel)
	Figaro Madame no. 14482 (France)	"La couleur c'est la vie" (Guillemette de Sairigné)
	Études rurales no. 117 (France)	"La géographie de la couleur" (Jean-Philippe Lenclos)
1992	*Glamour* no. 40 (France)	"La couleur et la mode"
	Automobiles classiques no. 48 (France)	"Les couleurs du Japon: echanges Paris-Tokyo" (Serge Bellu)
	Performances no. 2 (France)	"Jean-Philippe Lenclos aux sources de la couleur" (Martine Debaussart)
	The Colour of the City, Taverne & Cor Wagenaar (Netherlands)	"ISBN 90 74 265 03 0 GEB"
	L'Automobile magazine no. 555 (France)	"Entretien Jean-Philippe Lenclos: l'amoureux des couleurs" (Robert Gelly)
	Libération no. 2595	"Les villes françaises ne s'aiment pas en couleur" (Sibylle Vincendon)
	Design Magazine no. 527 (Great Britain)	"Natural selection trends colour" (Carl Gardner)
1993	*Urbanisme* no. 261 (France)	"Le voleur de couleurs" (Catherine Sabbah)
	BAT no. 152 (France)	"La couleur dominante" (Noëlle Gauthier)
	La Dépêche du Midi (France)	"Des goûts et des couleurs" (Gérard Santier)
	Chine Art Weerkle no. 1 (China)	"Un nouveau domaine: la géographie de la couleur" (Song Jian Ming)
	CAUS News (United States)	"CAUS holds conference on color in the year 2000"
	Routledge Companion to Architecture Thought (Great Britain)	"Architectural form and colour" (Tom Porter)
1994	*Daidalos* no. 51 (Germany)	"Die Geographie der Farbe" (Jean-Philippe Lenclos)
	Cosmetique News no. 190	"Jean-Philippe Lenclos: président, directeur, général de l'Atelier 3D Couleur" (Antigone Schilling)
	Color Forecasting, Van Nostrand Reinhold (United States)	"Trends, signs. and symbols" (Harold Linton)
	Journal du textile no. 2021 (France)	"L'air du temps flairé par les leaders d'opinion"
1995	*Car Styling* no. 104 (Japan)	"Trends in colors at the Mondial"
	Dizajn no. 2 (France)	"Un métier, une entreprise, un homme" (Dominique Wagner)
	D'A, Architectures no. 56 (France)	"Le voleur de couleurs" (Catherine Sabbah)
	Car Styling no. 107 (Japan)	"Product Color Dynamics" (Jean-Philippe Lenclos)
	Création no. 2 (China)	"Un coloriste français, Jean-Philippe Lenclos et son travail" (Song Jian Ming)
	Car Styling no. 108 (Japan)	"Color design for transportation" (Jean-Philippe Lenclos)
1996	*View on colour*	"Atelier Earth" (Liza Whrigt)
	Étapes géographiques (France)	"Réflexions chromatiques" (Bénédicte Le Guérinel)
	Journal de l'École nationale supérieure des arts décoratifs (France)	"Faire vivre la couleur"
		"La stratégie de la couleur à l'ENSAD"
	L'Entreprise (France)	"Les couleurs qui font vendre" (Pascale Poncelet)
	Colourscape (Great Britain)	"ISBN 1-85490-4315" (Michael Lancaster)
1997	*Le Revenu Français* (France)	"Un petit jaune sinon rien!" (Sabine Dreyfus)
	Dépêche Mode (France)	"Les couleurs qui font vendre" (Ph.-P. Adolphe, S. Chapuy)
	Marie-France (France)	"Des couleurs pour nous faire craquer" (I. Soing)
1998	*B&M 5. Architecture* (Belgium)	"Dialogues entre la couleur et l'architecture"
	Le Journal du dimanche (France)	"Le rouge est mis" (Caroline Tossan)
	Cosmétique News	Interview Portrait (Agnès Legiül)
1999	*Le Mobilier Français 1960–1998,* Edit. Massin (France)	"ISBN 2-7072-0338-6" (Yvonne Brunhammer, Marie-Laure Perrin)
	D'A, Architectures no. 90 (France)	"Couleur, l'importance du contexte" (Pascale Blin)
	La Tribune (France)	"La couleur permet de résister" (Sophie Seroussi)
	Colour Design in France, Shanghai, People's Fine Arts Publishing (China)	"ISBN 7-5322-2189-X/J-2069" (Song Jian Ming)
	Fashion Colour no. 3, Shanghai (China)	"Jean-Philippe Lenclos: maître de la couleur" (Jia Zong Li)
	Color in Architecture, McGraw-Hill (United States)	"ISBN-0-07-038119-4" "Design Methods for Buildings" (Harold Linton)

BIBLIOGRAPHY

BOOKS

Joseph Albers
Interaction of Color
New Haven, London, 1963

Antoñio Barbosa
Olinda 450 Anos Spala Editora
Rio de Janeiro, 1985

Damian Bayon and Murillio Marx
L'art Colonial Sud-Américain
Aurore Editions d'Art, Paris, 1990.

Jeffrey Becom and Sally Jean Aberg
Maya Color: The Painted Villages of Mesoamerica
Abbeville Press, New York, 1997

José-Marie Bel
Architecture et peuple du Yémen
Conseil International de la Langue Française, 1988

Fredy Bemont
Les villes de l'Iran: des cités d'autrefois à l'urbanisme contemporain
Paris, 1969–1973

Régis Bertrand and Danielle Magne
The Textiles of Guatemala
Studio Editions, London, 1991

Paul Bonnenfant
Les Maison-tours de Sana'a
CNRS, Paris, 1989

Clara Cardia
Ils ont construit New York: histoire de la métropole au XIXe siècle
Georg Editeur SA, Geneva, 1987

Paul Changion
The African Mural
Struik Publishers, Cape Town, 1989

Margaret Courtney-Clark
Ndebele: The Art of an African Tribe
Rizzoli International Publications, New York, 1986

Jean Dethier
Architectures de terre, ou l'avenir d'une tradition millénaire
Editions du Centre Pompidou, Paris, 1986

Henriette and Jean-Marc Didillon, Catherine and Pierre Donnadieu
Habiter le desert: les maisons Mozabites
Coll. Architecture et Recherches, Editions Pierre Mardaga, Brussels, 1977

Francis Dore
La Vie Indienne
Presses Universitaires de France, Paris, second edition, 1984

Didier Drummond
Architectes des favelas: les pratiques de l'espace
Bordas, Paris, 1981

Joanne Dunn
San Francisco: terre de tous les rêves
Editions Soline, Paris, 1991

Dominique Gauzin-Müller
Le Bois dans la construction
Editions du Moniteur, Paris, 1990

Paul Goldberger
The City Observed: New York, a Guide to the Architecture of Manhattan
Vintage Books, New York, 1979

Lucien Golvin and Marie-Christine Fromont
Thula: architecture et urbanisme
Editions Recherche sur les Civilisations, 1984

W.D. Hammond-Tooke
The Bantu-Speaking Peoples of Southern Africa
Routledge and Kegan Paul, London, 1974

Suzanne and Max Hirschi
L'Architecture au Yémen du Nord
Berger-Levrault, 1983

Ada Louise Huxtable
Classic New York
Anchor Books, United States, 1964

Teiji Itoh
Maisons anciennes au Japon
Office du Livre, Fribourg, 1983

D. Jacques-Meunié
Architectures et habitats du Dadès
Librairie C. Klincksieck, Paris, 1962

Michael Jenner
Yemen Rediscovered
Editions Longman, London (published in association with the Yemen Tourism Company)

Nishi and Hozumi Kazuo
What is Japanese Architecture?
Kodansha, London, 1996

Basile H. Kerblay
L'Isba d'hier et d'aujourd'hui
L'Age d'Homme, Lausanne, 1973

Michael Larsen and Elizabeth Pomada
Painted Ladies: Those Resplendent Victorians
Dutton, New York, 1978

Jean-Philippe and Dominique Lenclos
Couleurs de la France
Editions du Moniteur, Paris, 1982

Jean-Philippe and Dominique Lenclos
Couleurs de l'Europe
Editions du Moniteur, Paris, 1995

Jean-Philippe and Dominique Lenclos
Cité florale, itinéraire chromatique, hameaux, villas et cités de Paris
Action Artistique de la Ville de Paris, 1998

Harold Linton
Color Consulting: A Survey of International Color Design
Van Nostrand Reinhold, New York, 1991

Pascal and Maria Maréchaux
Yémen
Editions Phébus, 1994

Anna Mariani
Facades: maisons populaires du Nordeste
Editora Nova Fronteira SA, Rio de Janeiro, 1988

Tomoya Masuda
Architecture Universelle: Japon
Office du Livre, Fribourg, 1969

Rigoberta Menchù
I, Rigoberta Menchù: An Indian Woman in Guatemala
Chapman & Hall, New York, Routledge, 1985

Corinne and Laszlo Mester de Parajd
Regards sur l'habitat traditionnel au Niger
Editions Créer, France, 1988

Robert Montagne
Villages et kasbas Berbères, 1930

Mary H. Nooter
African Art That Conceals and Reveals
The Museum for African Art, New York, 1993

Pezeu-Massabuau
La Maison Japonaise
Publications Orientalistes de France, Paris, 1981

Tom Porter
Colour Outside
The Architectural Press, London, 1982

Ivor Powell
Ndebele: A People and Their Art
Cross River Press, New York, 1995

André Ravéreau
Le M'zab: une leçon d'architecture
Editions Sinbad, Paris, 1987

Manuelle Roche
Le M'zab: architecture Ibadite en Algérie
Editions Arthaud, 1970

Alain Rouaud
Les Yémen et leurs populations
Editions Complexe, Brussels, 1979

Nand Kishore Sharma
Jaisalmer: la ville dorée
Seemant Prakashan, Jaisalmer, India

Kishore Singh and Lewis Karoki
Jodhpur, Bikaner: les royaumes du désert
Lustre Press Pvt. Ltd., New Delhi, India, 1992

Henri Stierlin
Ispahan: image du paradis
Sigma, Geneva, 1976

Henri Terrasse
Kasbas Berbères
1938

Dominique Zahan
L'Homme et la couleur: histoire des moeurs
Encyclopédie de la Pléïade, Gallimard, Paris, 1990

Reviews

Hassan Fathy
AA, l'Architecture d'aujourd'hui, February 1978

Claudie Fayein
"La construction au Yémen"
Bâtir, November 1954

Song Jian Ming
"Le codage des couleurs dans l'architecture chinoise"
Pour la science, January 1993

Stephen P. Huyler
"L'instant sacré"
Le Courrier de l'UNESCO, December 1996

Tom Porter
"Colour in architecture"
Architectural Design, no. 120, London, 1996

"Terres et couleurs" no. 3
Paris, February 1998

Studies, Dissertations, Colloquium

Mohaman Haman
Le Bambou et la capacité locale d'initiative au Cameroun, séminaire international pour la sauvegarde et la promotion des techniques traditionnelles du bambou dans la vie moderne
Ho Chi Minh City, December 17–19, 1997

Le CRAterre (Centre de Recherche et d'Application)
Construire en terre
Alternative et Parallèles, Paris, 1979

Yves Leloup
Les Villes du Minas Gerais
Dissertation, University of Paris IV, 1969

AmaNdebele
Farbsignale aus Südafrika, Haus der Welt
Ernst Wasmuth Publisher Tübingen, Berlin, 1991

Les Portugais au Brésil
L'Art dans la vie quotidienne
Europalia, Portugal, 1994

Sima Hafezi-Kouban
Yazd: Face à la "modernisation"
Dissertation, Sociology, Paris VII, 1975

Display Catalogs

Courtyard
Musée National des Arts d'Afrique et d'Océanie, and Musée d'Art Moderne de Villeneuve d'Ascq, 1996

De Terre, de paille et de bois: symbolique de l'architecture en Afrique Noire
Musée de l'Homme, Paris, 1998

Sana'a: parcours d'une cité d'Arabie
Under the direction of Pascal Maréchaux, IMA
Institut du Monde Arabe, Paris, 1987

CREDITS

PHOTOGRAPHS

In this work, 478 photographs are by Jean-Philippe Lenclos;
the others were taken by:

Jean Bersoux	page 62, photos 1 and 2
Color Planning Center (Tokyo)	page 14, photos 1, 2, and 3
François Dejean	page 85, photo 2; page 91, photo 2
Eric Guillouard	page 28, photo 2; page 32, photo 4
Isabelle Jacquard	page 25
Thomas Klug	page 130, photo 2
Ubald Klug	page 15, photo 2; page 16, photo 2
Dominique Lenclos	page 27, photo 2; page 30, photo 4; page 34, photo 1; page 35, photos 1 and 2; page 41, photos 2, 3, and 4; page 42, photo 2; page 45, photo 2; page 47, photo 2; page 50, photo 1; page 51, photos 1, 2, and 3; page 54, photo 1; page 56, photos 1 and 2; page 59, photo 3; page 60, photo 2; page 64, photo 1; page 66, photos 3 and 4; page 67, photos 1 and 4; page 81, photo 1; page 113, photo 3; page 114, photo 2; page 118, photo 1; page 121, photo 1; page 124, photos 1, 2, 3, and 4; page 147, photo 1; page 54, photos 1, 2, and 3; page 155, photos 1, 3, 4, and 5; page 156, photos 1, 2, 3, 4, 5, 6, 7, and 8; page 162, photo 4; page 166, photo 1; page 167, photo 1; page 168, photos 1, 2, 3, and 4; page 169, photos 1, 2, 3, and 4; page 175, photos 1 and 2; page 224, photo 1; page 225, photo 3; page 226, photos 1 and 2; page 227, photo 3; page 260, photo 1; page 261, photos 1 and 2; page 263, photo 2
Rudi Meyer	page 19
René Robert	pages 4, 21, 23, 71, and 136

REPRODUCTIONS

Color Planning Center (Tokyo)	page 14
Jean-Philippe Lenclos	page 63: 5; page 206: 1; page 210: 1; page 215: 3
René Robert	pages 20, 22, and 23; page 68: A, B, and C; page 69: 1, 2, and 3; page 70: 1, 2, 3, and 4; page 83: 1 and 2; page 84: 1; page 111: 1, 2, 3, 4, 5, and 6; page 96: 1 and 2: page 117; page 127: 1; page 128: 3; page 130: 1; page 136: 1, 2, and 3; page 150: 1; page 176: 1; page 177: 1; page 189: 1 and 2; page 201: 1; page 203: 2; page 277: 1; page 280: 1

ILLUSTRATIONS

Jean-Philippe Lenclos	page 17; page 63: 5; page 96: 3 and 4; page 137: 1; page 176: 1; page 189: 3
Fabrice Moireau	page 98, 110, 126, 144, 157, 188, 202, 217, 231, 282
Jean-Jacques Terrin	page 117

CHARTS AND SYNTHESIS

Atelier 3D Couleur	page 18; page 20; page 21; page 22: 3; page 23; page 111; page 136; page 189: 1 and 2; page 217: 1, 2, 3, and 4
Agnès Decourchelle	page 69
Béatrice Kluge	page 68
Marie Lenclos	page 22: 1 and 2; page 150: 1; page 201: 1; page 203: 2; page 232: 1; page 252: 1; page 245: 2 and 3
Christopher Roger	page 277: 1

CARTOGRAPHY

All geographic maps in this book were designed by Rudi Meyer